MW00989897

A History of Hollywood's Outsourcing Debate

A History of Hollywood's Outsourcing Debate

Runaway Production

Camille Johnson-Yale

LEXINGTON BOOKS
Lanham • Boulder • New York • London

Published by Lexington Books
An imprint of The Rowman & Littlefield Publishing Group, Inc.
4501 Forbes Boulevard, Suite 200, Lanham, Maryland 20706
www.rowman.com

Unit A, Whitacre Mews, 26-34 Stannary Street, London SE11 4AB

British Library Cataloguing in Publication Information Available

Library of Congress Cataloging-in-Publication Data Available

ISBN 9781498532532 (cloth : alk. paper)
ISBN 9781498532549 (electronic)

∞™ The paper used in this publication meets the minimum requirements of American National Standard for Information Sciences—Permanence of Paper for Printed Library Materials, ANSI/NISO Z39.48-1992.

Printed in the United States of America

In memory of my dad,
Gary L. Johnson (1939–2015)

Contents

Acknowledgments

This book would not have been possible without the support and generosity of several people. First and foremost, I owe a debt of gratitude to my advisor and friend, John Nerone, Professor Emeritus of Communications at the University of Illinois at Urbana–Champaign. His patience, insight, and humor served as a lifeline throughout the development and completion of this research. I would also like to extend a special thanks to Steve Jones, Distinguished Professor of Communication at University of Illinois in Chicago, for being a committed and inspiring mentor, and setting me on the path of my academic career.

While compiling my research, I visited several film industry archives, and had the privilege of working with some of the best research librarians in the field. As such, I wish to extend my deepest gratitude to Barbara Hall at the Margaret Herrick Library of the Academy of Motion Picture Arts and Sciences, Ned Comstock at the University of Southern California Cinematic Arts Library, Kris Kasianovitz and Julie Graham at UCLA's Arts Special Collections Library, and the numerous and incredibly knowledgeable research assistants at the California State Archives in Sacramento and the Wisconsin Center for Film and Theater Research at the Wisconsin Historical Society in Madison.

And finally, I wish to express my infinite appreciation and love for my husband, Rob, and my son, Wes. Rob also served as an invaluable consultant to this research, drawing on over twenty years' experience working in Chicago's television and film production industries. For these things, and much more, I am eternally grateful.

Introduction to a Critical History of Runaway Production

In 1930, Frances Taylor Patterson wrote an article for *The New Republic* in which she considered the most appropriate home for the fast-developing American motion picture industry. She made her pitch for Broadway, arguing that New York's world-famous theater district could provide the film industry with the "talking" actors it so desperately needed as it transitioned from silent to sound production. Broadway also had a proven track record, with over 100 years of producing high quality entertainment compared to Hollywood's tenuous 20-year run. To those who saw Hollywood as the authentic home of the motion picture industry, Patterson offered the following response:

> The natives of Hollywood are not the moving picture industry; they merely serve it. They feed it, they clothe it, they house it, and they make it beautiful. The industry itself is a trouper. If it sees a chance for a better stand somewhere else, it will pull up stakes and move forthwith. . . . Hollywood wouldn't be the first town to be developed and then abandoned by industry; nor would it be the first expensive 'set' that the film folk have built, used briefly, and then demolished. (Patterson, 1930, p. 298)

While the far-flung lemon groves of southern California would ultimately be transformed into the epicenter of global motion picture production, Patterson's assessment of the industry was not completely off base. On the one hand, she correctly understood film production to be an industry like many others, with practical considerations to be made and needs to be met for it to succeed. Patterson also recognized that film production was a capricious, excessive, and mobile industry in ways perhaps foreign to stage production, with the production process being a means to an end (a film) rather than the end itself (a stage play). Despite understanding the ways that film and stage productions were fundamentally different, Patterson could not see how this also made Broadway a completely inflexible and unsuitable home for film production. She did not see how the self-serving mobility of the industry could also work against Broadway's bid: if the film production industry and the resources it required could be moved to Broadway as she suggested, then certainly they could be moved to Hollywood away from Broadway as well. And as history would illustrate, no other film production resource was more mobile than people, including Broadway's stage actors in the 1930s, who gladly hopped on trains headed for the West Coast, some never to return to New York's theater district.

It is evident that by 1930, a debate over film industry competition and ownership was underway. And by the standards of the Great Depression, the fledgling film industry must have seemed like an economic prize worth fighting for: in 1930, roughly 80 million Americans attended movies each week, generating domestic box office revenues of $723 million. As an employment sector the film industry also showed promise, with 143,000 reportedly working in the industry in 1930 (Show Business: It Just Ain't So, 1980), a number that surpassed employment figures for gas works (115,000) but still paled in comparison to industrial behemoths such as the commercial railroads (1.5 million) (U.S. Bureau of the Census, 1930).

More than eighty years later, the U.S. motion picture and television industries have become their own industrial behemoths, making significant revenue and trade contributions to the U.S. economy, as well as functioning as a major domestic employment sector. Domestic box office revenues (United States and Canada) hit a record $11 billion in 2015, with an additional $27 billion in worldwide ticket sales (Motion Picture Association of America, 2015, p. 4). The Motion Picture Association of America has also reported that 1.9 million private sector jobs can be attributed to film and television industries: 653,000 directly related to the production, marketing, manufacturing, and distribution of TV and film products, and another 1.2 million jobs supported through indirect services to media industries, such as lumber sales, catering, hotels, and restaurants. Though California continues to host the largest concentration of domestic media production labor, 50 percent of all industry jobs can now be found in other states, including large and active workforces in New York, Illinois, Louisiana, and Florida (Motion Picture Association of America, 2015, p. 2). On a global scale, audiovisual service exports, which include motion picture and television programs,[1] consistently produce trade surpluses, topping $13 billion in 2014, and exceeding surpluses generated by other major economic sectors including telecommunications and insurance services (p. 5).

With such incredible economic rewards at stake, competition for media industry dollars has only continued to escalate since the early part of the twentieth century. Hollywood television and film production are now global enterprises, owned and managed by multinational media corporations with the power to negotiate optimal political and economic conditions for the production and distribution of their products. But as we've seen with other major U.S. industries, including automobile production, market expansion of film and television industries has not served everyone's interests equally. While industry owners and proponents of free trade have reveled in the opening of lucrative markets abroad, Hollywood production labor has lamented the impact that domestic and foreign industry investments have had on their job security—a complaint that has been organized within the issue of runaway production, the subject of this book.

RUNAWAY PRODUCTION: AN INTRODUCTION

Runaway production is a phrase commonly used by Hollywood film and television production labor to describe the outsourcing of production work to foreign locations. It is an issue that has been credited with siphoning tens of millions of dollars and thousands of jobs from the U.S. economy. As a political platform, runaway production has inspired numerous Congressional hearings, a special report by the Commerce Department, and tax initiatives in nearly every state in the United States. Runaway production has also been extensively discussed, and sometimes lampooned, in the popular and trade press, and has served as the subject of numerous academic journal articles and books on the global film industry. But despite broad interest in runaway production and its potential impact on hundreds of thousands of workers employed directly and indirectly in U.S. media industries, there has been very little critical analysis of its historical development or its cultural implications.

Through extensive archival research, this book critically examines the history of runaway production, from its origins in postwar recovery politics in the 1940s to its appearance in more recent debates over "corporate welfare" and state-funded industry subsidies. But rather than revealing a singular narrative of economic outsourcing of film and television production work from the United States, this research describes the multiple meanings and uses that have been applied to runaway production over the last sixty years: in the 1950s and 1960s, runaway productions could be film projects lured away from the United States by blacklisted Hollywood talent exiled in Europe, or a descriptor for domestic productions staged outside the jurisdiction of Hollywood's unions, or as a production phenomenon spurred by the lifestyle choices of Hollywood's globe-trotting and capricious elite. In the 1970s and beyond, runaway production could refer to the outsourcing of a specific production process, like ink and paint for animation or computer-generated special effects, or domestic production work "running" from state to state, or as an economic consequence of NAFTA, with Canada and Mexico being the beneficiaries of runaway productions.

At first glance, the many historical transformations of the meaning of runaway production all seem to point toward one creeping reality: that Hollywood and the U.S. production industries are reacting to a loss of authority over a globalizing industry. However, I take an opposite stance in this book, arguing that the multiple, historical meanings of runaway production have worked together to reinforce what Stuart Hall (1996) described as a "regime of truth"; in this case, an understanding of Hollywood as the authentic home to global film production, and all others as its inauthentic, even criminal, harborers. In many ways, runaway production relies on the powerful metaphor and moral tale of the "runaway" made famous by Hollywood movies like *The Wizard of Oz* (1939) as its central construct: a naïve and willful child (i.e., Hollywood production) is lured away from a loving home by the prospect of adventure and streets paved with gold. But what the "runaway" finds instead is that things aren't what they appear to be; that life on the road is full of obstacles and fanciful, inauthentic representations of real places, people, and experiences. And that in the end, there's no place like home—and no production location like Hollywood. Few would refute the historical importance and political and economic prowess of Hollywood to film and television production industries. But it is the claim that this prowess makes Hollywood the most authentic production location—its natural home—and all others a cheap imitation of Hollywood, that forms a core logic and point of disjuncture within the regime of truth proposed by the discourse of runaway production.

Debates over authentic and inauthentic production communities have their place in the development of globalizing industries. Media economist Susan Christopherson (2005) has argued that divisive issues such as runaway production ultimately complement the "divide and conquer," anti-union labor strategies commonly implemented by multinational corporations (MNCs). This specifically involves the use of industry subsidies by MNCs to create competition between dispersed labor forces, locking these groups into a classic "race to the bottom" as they try to undercut one another to attract lucrative film and television projects. Though runaway production has been primarily identified as a labor discourse, the historical record presented in this book shows how runaway production has also clearly served the hegemonic interests of multinational media corporations. As Doreen Massey (1984) has argued, the power-geometry of the new global economy hinges on the mobilization and de-territorialization of industry and its production processes while at the same time isolating and immobilizing unionized labor. In the case of runaway production, we see a history in which Hollywood's multinational giants, including the likes of Warner Brothers and the Walt Disney Company, successfully transformed a production process bound to studios and their affiliated unions in the early 1900s into a highly mobile and adaptable industry that can escape Hollywood union contracts and instead travel to locations anywhere around the globe, be it Wilmington, North Carolina or Auckland, New Zealand, offering the lowest labor costs and the largest subsidy packages. The result is a Hollywood labor diaspora: a globally dispersed labor force bound by a common cultural identity as Hollywood labor, while also divided by their differing labor histories as well as their unequal relationship to the discursive mythology of Hollywood as the industry's authentic homeland.

A study of runaway production encompasses several areas of scholarly inquiry in media and communication research, including media history, labor and industry studies, theories of space and mobility, and theories of culture and discourse. As mentioned previously, there is also a growing interest in the issue of runaway production from other scholarly fields including political science, law, and economics. The research presented here combines media history and media industry studies, while also relating to more contemporary studies of discourses of economy and globalization. It is my hope that this book can make a substantive contribution to existing studies of runaway production that have yet to fully explore and contextualize its historical development, or problematize the assumptions and worldviews inherent within the phrase runaway production.

It is important to preface a more in-depth discussion of runaway production with an orientation toward the organizational structure of Hollywood, particularly its diverse labor force, as many of the disjunctures that have formed within globalizing media industries have occurred along the fault lines of the division and distribution of cultural labor. Media production industries employ a vast spectrum of workers, from the most high-profile and high-powered actors, directors, and producers, to the thousands of skilled and semi-skilled laborers that work behind the scenes. One of the basic industry structures that proves integral to the history of runaway production is the delineation of labor into "above-the-line" and "below-the-line" job sectors. The phrases "above-" and "below-the-line" first refer to an industry division of production expenses, which are secondarily applied to the labor that fit into their respective expense categories. Above-the-line costs typically encompass script development and other creative expenses, including producers, writers, directors, and actors (usually the stars or "hero" talent, and not secondary or background performers). The unions and guilds affiliated with above-the-line workers include the Screen Actors Guild (SAG), the Directors Guild of America (DGA), the Writers Guild of America (WGA), the Alliance of Motion

Picture and Television Producers (AMPTP), as well as the now-defunct Society of Independent Motion Picture Producers (SIMPP) (Wasko, 2003).

Conversely, below-the-line costs apply to the more technical and hands-on aspects of production and post production, such as lighting, transportation, equipment rental, wardrobe, editing, and set construction. The largest population of film and television workers identified as below-the-line belong to the International Alliance of Theatrical and Stage Employees (IATSE, or IA), and include, but are by no means limited to, grips, set dressers, makeup artists, wardrobe stylists, editors, special effects technicians, property masters, scenic painters, and construction laborers. While IA members typically comprise the production crews for motion pictures, television series, commercials, and made-for-TV movies, the National Association of Broadcast Employees and Technicians (NABET) represents technical crew members working in broadcast and cable television, particularly news production. Finally, the International Brotherhood of Teamsters is also categorized as below-the-line labor, with 4,000 drivers and security staff registered with the Hollywood Local alone (Wasko, 2003, p. 47). The history of Hollywood's unions is rife with turmoil, which often centered on jurisdictional feuds between below-the-line unions, strikes against major studios, and industry upheaval over the threat of communist infiltration of the motion picture industry and its unions (Horne, 2001; Ross, 1941). And as you might expect, these issues also accentuated labor differentials in the industry, particularly as they related to class and privilege. And as Steven Ross (1998) has argued, class differentials behind the camera became were also increasingly evident in the films that were being made, as movies centered on the lives of the working class were gradually replaced with films about the middle class.

Above- and below-the-line labor have often ended up on opposite sides of industry debates, and the issue of runaway production has been no exception. A primary reason for this split has been the differential effects of location shooting on above- and below-the-line labor. In almost all cases, key actors, directors, and writers are considered irreplaceable labor that must travel with productions, while below-the-line labor have more often been considered interchangeable, with most set labor hired on location. John Sullivan (2008) argues that "making of" featurettes included on movie DVDs serve as explicit evidence of this Hollywood labor hierarchy, as they almost exclusively focus on the experiences of above-the-line talent, erasing the presence and contributions of below-the-line labor. A secondary reason for the division of interests can be attributed to pay structure. Most above-the-line labor, including members of the Writers', Actors', and Directors' Guilds, are paid a negotiated percentage from the exhibition and syndication revenues of film and television programs, called residuals or royalties. This pay stipulation has been fiercely protected by above-the-line guilds in their contract negotiations with the Alliance of Motion Picture and Television Producers (AMPTP) and has often served as an impetus for strikes, including the 2007–2008 WGA strike over residuals for new media distribution of television and film. However, below-the-line workers are typically paid an hourly "card" rate and excluded from the more lucrative residuals pay system. Subsequently, resentments have festered between the two labor factions as below-the-line labor have been necessarily affected by the frequent work stoppages staged by above-the-line labor over residuals, but receive no direct benefit from any residual increases resulting from the stoppages (Caldwell, 2008).

With a narrow focus on labor and production costs, it is perhaps no surprise runaway production has primarily been approached as an economic phenomenon. Researchers in the areas of business and law have treated runaway production as a case of industry outsourcing, considering its impact on unemployment in Los Angeles as well as the economic stability of California's production industry (Conley Ulich & Simmens, 2001; Randle & Culkin, 2005). Similarly, media historians and political economists have treated the subject as one of many economic conditions signaling an increase in foreign investment and globalization of the Hollywood film industry beginning in the post-war era (Balio, 1976; Guback, 1969). More recently, economic geographers have predicted a continued intensification of production outsourcing from Hollywood. Specifically, high-budget runaway films such as *The Lord of the Rings* and *Hobbit Trilogies* (New Zealand), *The Matrix* (Australia), and *Cold Mountain* (Romania) are argued to represent a globally expanding network of Hollywood locations that pose a challenge to even the most successful North American runaway locations, namely Vancouver, B.C. (Scott, 2005; Scott, 2002; Scott & Pope, 2007). Economist Susan Christopherson has been one of the most prolific researchers in media labor and globalization (Christopherson, 2005; Christopherson, 2009; Christopherson & Clark, 2007; Christopherson & Rightor, 2010). Specifically, Christopherson looks at the unique conditions of film and television production and their impact on global divisions of labor and capital mobility. Since the mid-1980s, she has consistently argued that the issue of runaway production should be understood as a labor reaction to two distinct economic processes within the globalizing film industry: the fragmentation of "routine" and specialized production practices, and the fostering of inter-regional competition and divisiveness among workforces by transnational media corporations, a tactic she calls "divide and conquer" (Christopherson & Clark, 2007, p. 103; Christopherson & Storper, 1989). In this way, Christopherson shares a view of globalization processes held by other media industry scholars (i.e., Appadurai, 1996 and Miller et al., 2001), in that she sees multiple industry factors (e.g., labor, capital, government policy, corporate interests) being engaged across multiple geographic planes (e.g., local, regional, national, transnational).

Critical media scholars have looked at runaway production due to the increasingly cozy relationships between multinational media corporations and various government entities around the globe. Miller and Leger (2001) have argued that Hollywood has worked in tandem with the "Washington Consensus" to promote a neoliberal global trade agenda. Some countries like Canada have attempted to protect their indigenous media industries against a U.S. media deluge by arguing for exemptions of cultural products from their free trade agreements with the United States. However, Miller and Leger argue that Hollywood has been engaged in "major governmental and business assaults on the legitimacy of national self-determination undertaken by other countries to utilize state support to generate and sustain cultural industries" (p. 91). As Hollywood has attempted to expand its distribution horizon overseas, a "network of practices and institutions" have been utilized to soften stubborn markets, including the technical training of local labor for use on co-productions in the host country. Far from being a recent development, the recruitment and training of local labor has been going on since just after World War II, coinciding with the first mentions of runaway production among Hollywood film labor (Miller, 2003, p. 134; Miller, Govil, McMurria, & Maxwell, 2001; Miller & Leger, 2001). The result has been a New International Division of Cultural Labor (NICL), a theory which reconciles the importance of "'flexible' cultural labor to the new global cultural economy" (Miller & Leger, 2001, p. 90).

Throughout this book, the NICL is used as a key construct for discussing the shifting power dynamics between above- and below-the-line labor within the discourse of runaway production. The NICL describes the differential distribution and mobility of cultural labor in the service of transnational industries, including Hollywood film production. As previously explained, above-the-line labor has tended to be the more mobile labor force, travelling with productions no matter how far flung their locations. Below-the-line labor, on the other hand, has tended to be the more stationary workforce. While jobs such as lighting technicians, set construction workers, or craft service workers may require a unique skill set, these jobs don't carry the name recognition of above-the-line jobs, and they are also typically paid by daily or hourly rates. In short, the idea of travelling below-the-line workers to locations is considered financially impractical, when skilled workers can be found (or trained) on-site, and perhaps at a lower rate than Hollywood's unionized labor. But as Massey (1984) has explained, it is not only the mobility of labor, but also the ability of certain strata of labor to exercise power over capital distribution and the means of production that create imbalances in all manner of globalizing production industries. In the case of Hollywood labor, above-the-line interests have had the upper hand within the NICL, with the ability to influence production locations based on the creative needs of directors, the financial needs of producers, the social and political needs of movie stars, and so on. Meanwhile, the influence of below-the-line Hollywood laborers over such processes has been systematically diminished since the end of World War II; the mass adoption of television and the 1948 Paramount Decision had profound effects on the organization and economics of Hollywood production practices during this time.

While the global economic practices of Hollywood have certainly dominated studies of runaway production, there are some that have examined the cultural and historical significance of the issue as well. Elmer and Gasher's (2005) edited collection, *Contracting Out Hollywood* provides an array of essays on the subject, including the impact of runaway production on the construction of narrative and aesthetic forms, audience reception of runaway films, experiences of runaway production communities both inside and outside the United States, and case studies of the production of specific runaway films and television programs (p. 2). Of note is Matheson's (2005) chapter on the reproduction and experience of place and "placelessness" in runaway productions. She describes how both Canadian audiences and the Canadian film community embraced the ambiguously located and American-funded TV program *Night Heat* as their own, largely because it was filmed in Toronto. Serra Tinic (2006) has written a similar account of the experiences of cultural identity in Vancouver's television production industry. I expand upon Matheson and Tinic's discussions of the relationship between Canadian national identity, their indigenous media industries, and runaway production in chapter 4, where I provide a detailed history of Canada's counter-discourse to Hollywood's claims of runaway production.

A few historical studies have been undertaken, but overall, their scope is limited. For instance, Stubbs (2008) provides an interesting case study of the making of *Captain Horatio Hornblower* in 1951, and accusations of runaway production that occurred when Warner Brothers made the decision to film the movie in France and the UK rather than Hollywood. A more comprehensive history of runaway production can be found in Andrew Dawson's (2006) article titled "Bring Hollywood Home!: Studio Labor, Nationalism and Internationalism, and Opposition to 'Runaway Production,'" published in the Belgian academic journal *Revue Belge de Philologie et de Histoire*. In his twenty-page treatment of the subject, Dawson compares what he describes as the two most defined periods of runaway production resistance in Hollywood: the 1957–1965 anti-runaway labor campaign, characterized by McCarthyist politics and jingoism, and the 1999–2003 campaign that relied on the rhetoric of anti-free trade and fair trade practices. Dawson identifies European "frozen funds" production as the main impetus for runaway productions in the post-war period, and identifies some of the key players and events that defined the Hollywood anti-runaway production labor movement of the 1940s through the 1960s, most notably the anti-communist and anti-runaway production activities of Hollywood IA and AFL Film Council president Roy Brewer. Dawson also makes mention of intermediate developments in the fight against runaway production in the 1970s, specifically the animation guild's successfully negotiated "runaway clause."

While the body of research on runaway production continues to grow, it is evident that much of the existing work has shied away from an in-depth history, and has instead focused on mapping certain labor strategies and policy initiatives taken on by Hollywood's unions in the last twenty-five years. Alternately, the existing research has focused on bounded case studies where the primary concern has been to understand the ways that local production workers and audiences are making meaning from their experiences of runaway production. And yet this research stops short of probing the ideological underpinnings of runaway production as a culturally-situated and productive discourse. While the United States has a long history of promoting global free trade and resisting any limitations that might be imposed on this process, many other countries look at media products such as TV shows and movies as cultural products, worthy of special conditions and protections in trade agreements. In this clash of interests over the last seventy years, questions have been raised concerning the rights of certain communities to claim ownership over the production and reproduction of their culture in the media, the right to be a part of the production of the media they consume, even if it doesn't specifically depict their culture, as well as the right to institute subsidies and incentives in the interest of more equitable free trade conditions. It is a critical analytical omission found in the existing research on runaway production, and one that I hope to shed light on in the critical history of runaway production presented in this book.

Another limitation is that existing studies of runaway production have tended to approach the subject as an empirically valid phenomenon, focusing on the economic plight of Hollywood and U.S. media labor in the wake of ever-escalating production outsourcing. But few, if any, have turned their analytical focus back on runaway production as a discursive phenomenon, despite its highly protectionist and imperialistic connotations. I would argue that this is in large part due to the general treatment of economic issues, including employment trends, as self-evident and valid, when in fact they are anything but this. In *New Keywords* (Bennett, Grossberg, Morris & Williams, 2005), J. K. Gibson-Graham describes the social shift from thinking about economy as managed by people in society to thinking about society as managed by economy, with the result being that "the economic imaginary has lost its discursive mandate and become an objective reality" (p. 96). Similarly, David Ruccio (2008) has noted the ambiguities and disjunctures that plague contemporary discourses and representations of economy, particularly among academics approaching the subject from outside the field of economics. Rather than attempting to verify the most accurate of these representations, Ruccio argues that we should critically examine their consequences "in terms of reproducing and strengthening the existing economic and social institutions and of imagining and generating new ones" (p. 7). In this sense, I have followed Gibson-Graham and Ruccio's lead, treating runaway production as an evolving set of discursive truths that have at once challenged and reproduced dominant political and economic ideologies inherent within the globalizing Hollywood film and television industries since World War II. Having been put forward primarily by academics in the United States and the U.K., these ideologies have naturally invoked the primacy of social democracy and global capitalism.

Modes of Production

At the heart of modern debates over outsourcing, regardless of the industry, are issues involving the management of production practices and labor across space and time. It is typically argued that over the last 100 years, Western societies have been in the process of transitioning from a Fordist mode of economy and production to a post-Fordist mode. In the early part of the twentieth century, the Ford Motor Company was perfecting the production of its wildly popular Model T by utilizing assembly lines and modern machinery to quickly produce large quantities of affordable cars (Allen, 1996, p. 281). Subsequently, the Fordist mode of production has become synonymous with certain characteristics of modern society, including the vertical integration of manufacturing industries, stable markets controlled by oligopolistic interests, scientific and technological progress, rationality, and the routinization and disciplining of labor practices (Storper, 1994, p. 195). All these factors combined are said to produce economies of scale, in which production costs decrease, the quantity of available goods increases, and the demand for goods also increases as more people have expendable income from their jobs in various sectors of industrial production—a self-sustaining system.

The emergence of the Hollywood film industry coincides with the beginning of the Fordist industrial era, as early industry giants including Charlie Chaplin and Cecille B. DeMille set up their studios in and around Los Angeles between 1913 and 1917. The Hollywood studio era of the 1920s and 1930s is often described as having instituted Fordist assembly-line techniques to the production of films, though there is some debate within industry studies whether the description has been appropriately applied. During this era, films often relied on predictable storylines and certain routinized production practices, including the use of soundstages, which some have argued established a classical Hollywood style that has endured as the industry has globalized (Bordwell, Staiger & Thompson, 1985). However, no two films were truly identical in the way that cars or other mass-produced consumer goods could be (Smith, 1998, p. 8). And yet other factors clearly demonstrated a Fordist mode of production at work in Hollywood, not the least of which was the overwhelming, oligopolistic grip that the studios had on the production and distribution of films in the United States. In 1944, Hollywood's "Big Five," which included Paramount, RKO, Warner Bros., Fox Films, and Loew's/MGM, dominated the domestic film market: their films represented nearly three quarters of all films viewed by Americans at that time, while nearly 25 percent of domestic theaters were also owned and operated by the same studios (Storper, 1994, p. 203; Waterman, 1982, p. 16). The success of Hollywood was also dependent on the shift in mass consumption practices characteristic of the Fordist economic turn, as the industry relied on a large, middle-class audience with money and time to spend on leisure activities like movie-going.

Fordism is a system that works best when it is centrally coordinated (e.g., Detroit as the power center of U.S. auto production), and when the types of goods being produced are relatively standardized (as opposed to customizable). Since the early-to-mid 1970s, however, the organization of industrial production and consumer markets have undergone distinct changes, which some argue are indicative of a new, post-Fordist industrial era (Amin, 1994). Centralized modes of production have been increasingly challenged by the decentralization of production within globalizing industries. As such, American industrial giants like Ford must now compete against globally dispersed competitors for market dominance, both domestically and overseas. Advances in production technologies have also increased the possibility of flexible modes of production, where manufacturers can more easily engage in small batch production to satisfy specialized consumer markets around the globe (Piore & Sabel, 1984). And not surprisingly, we see many examples of flexible specialization in our current information economy. For instance, Apple iPhones can be made to order and shipped to consumers anywhere there is mail service, or a TV show like *House of Cards* can be developed by data mining the media interests and viewing habits of a specific audience of Netflix subscribers. The dominance of media and communication technologies companies like Apple and Netflix have been used to support the argument that our society has entered a post-industrial economic era, dominated by the production, distribution, and consumption of information.

The theorized emergence of a post- or neo-Fordist mode of production in Hollywood serves as an interesting explanatory device, in terms of when and why the discourse of runaway production first appeared. But it is important to note that there is a great deal of disagreement within media industry studies as to whether this transition has in fact occurred. For those who support the idea of a transition to a post-Fordist mode of production in Hollywood, they point to the 1948 *U.S. vs. Paramount* anti-trust case (a.k.a. "The Paramount Decision"). The anti-trust ruling effectively dismantled the Big Five's oligopolistic stranglehold over the distribution and exhibition of films in the United States Storper (1994) argues that at this crucial point in the industry's history, the major studios were forced to shift to a system of flexible specialization. A defining characteristic of flexible specialization within the film industry, according to Storper, was the shift toward more competitive, yet cooperative, production practices. This included increased collaboration between the studios and independent production companies, which allowed the studios to rid themselves of some of the burdensome overhead costs of in-house production. The shift toward more competitive industry practices naturally brought major changes for film production labor. Under the studio system, the Big Five had attempted to monopolize the labor market by putting actors, writers, producers, directors, and skilled production labor under long-term exclusive contracts. After the Paramount Decision, the studios ended the practice of signing exclusive contracts with labor, and instead took their chances on hiring labor and talent on the open market (Gomery, 1986). For movie stars and other much-sought-after above-the-line talent, it was a veritable boon, as they could demand much more lucrative per-project contracts when freed from their stagnant studio contract salaries. Below-the-line workers, on the other hand, were at a distinct disadvantage outside the studio system, with Hollywood's craft unions reduced to the role of "hiring halls" at the mercy of the cost-conscious independents (p. 206). Unmoored from their home in the studios, it is at this juncture that labor used the phrase, runaway production, to express their frustration.

Storper has been accused of being overly selective in his account of Hollywood's transition to a post-Fordist mode of production. Instead, Smith (1998) contends that the Hollywood film industry has shown distinct signs of vertical reintegration in the 1980s and 1990s, and that it is too soon to declare that the industry has moved beyond Fordist models of industry organization and control. By Smith's account, and other prominent film industry scholars including Tino Balio, Hollywood is still comprised of a small group of massive media conglomerates, with oligopolistic control over certain sectors of the industry, specifically finance and distribution. As such, Smith suggests that it is perhaps better to understand Hollywood's contemporary mode of production as quasi-Fordist, or as David Harvey (1990) would describe it, "late capitalist": while certain elements of production and consumption have become more fragmented with the globalization of the Hollywood film industry, there still remains a great concentration of power and control within Hollywood, in terms of capital accumulation, ability to reproduce and broadly disseminate a Hollywood film aesthetic, as well as dominance of technological innovation within the industry. This final explanation seems to make the most sense within the history of runaway film production presented in this book. The concentration of power and control over the New International Division of Cultural Labor, and thus over the distribution of production and labor, has shown no signs of weakening over the last seventy years.

Globalizing Media Industries

In the past, theories of media and globalization were dominated by the concept of cultural imperialism, in which media and cultural products were argued to flow from a Western-dominated center to a non-Western periphery. The secondary recipients of Western media were then argued to be in danger of losing their localized cultural identity, and localized media, under this deluge of Western cultural influence. Much has changed in scholarly thinking about globalization and the role of media, with many media and communication scholars now supporting models that represent more complex, multidirectional global flows of cultural influence and capital. And rather than models that depict a flow of influence from the more modern West to "the Rest," contemporary theories of media and globalization consider the ways that multiple modernities may coexist and interact in a globalizing world (Appadurai, 1996; Hall, 1996; Harvey, 1990).

One of the most influential contemporary models of globalization, and one that serves as a foundation for this study of runaway production, is Arjun Appadurai's (1996) theory of global "scapes." Within this model, Appadurai identifies five major landscapes or dimensions that he sees as most important to shaping cultural, political, and economic experiences of globalization: 1) ethnoscapes, representing globally mobile groups and individuals, including guest workers, tourists, and immigrants; 2) mediascapes, comprised of both the electronic means of media and information distribution, as well as their content; 3) technoscapes, which include "both high and low, both mechanical and informational" technologies capable of traversing global boundaries at high speeds; 4) financescapes, characterized by transnational pooling and global flows of capital; and finally, 5) ideoscapes, made up of "the ideologies of states and the counterideologies of movements explicitly oriented to capturing state power or a piece of it...[consisting of] chains of ideas, terms, and images, including *freedom, welfare, rights, sovereignty, representation,* and the master term *democracy*" (pp. 33–36). Appadurai's scapes are argued to represent many of the key components and disjunctures within the historical debates over runaway production, including matters of mobile and immobile labor forces and production processes (i.e., ethnoscape, mediascape, technoscape), foreign investment and the fairness of free trade policies and cultural industry subsidies (i.e., financescape), and the political, economic, and cultural ideologies used both to defend and challenge production outsourcing (i.e., ideoscape).

While Appadurai's work provides a new way to map globalization, theories specifically addressing labor mobility, spatial distribution, and situated cultural identities also form an important part of the theoretical foundation of this book. A central logic within the discourse of runaway production is arguably the loss of territorial ownership and cultural identity by the Hollywood production industry. Canclini's (1995) work proves useful in this regard, particularly his discussion of the de-territorialization of cultural identity in a global context. For Canclini, de-territorialization is a discourse used to express ''the loss of the 'natural' relation of culture to geographical and social territories'' (1995, p. 229). Similarly, it is argued that the discourse of runaway production has been used by Hollywood labor to describe the loss of a natural relationship between media (i.e., cultural) production and its geographic "homeland" in Southern California. Alternately, theories of re-territorialization and "corporate transculturalism" (Kraidy, 2005) describe cultural discourses "in which fluid identities and porous cultural borders are depicted as growth engines in service of a cosmopolitan capitalism'' (p. 90). This perspective proves particularly relevant within counter discourses to runaway production, as producers and other free trade interests reprimand Hollywood production labor for their old-fashioned and short-sighted understanding of the political economy of global Hollywood.

QUESTIONS AND METHODS

Several questions have guided this historical examination of runaway production. Most centrally, I have sought to understand the function of runaway production for the Hollywood industry and its labor, as well as its function within, and compatibility with, more overarching political, economic, and cultural contexts. For instance, how has the discourse of runaway production reinforced Hollywood's claim to being the authentic home of global film production? How has it challenged or perhaps reinforced dominant political and economic ideologies at various points in Hollywood's history, such as anti-communism during the highly public House Un-American Activities Committee Hearings? And finally, how has runaway production, and its construction of Hollywood as the authentic home of film and television production, been understood or perhaps challenged by production interests in so-called runaway locations? The underlying contention in these questions is that runaway production, and perhaps other pro-labor movements, can take on a hegemonic function, ultimately fostering programs such as industry tax breaks that paradoxically reinforce and even reward the neoliberal globalization that below-the-line labor have opposed.

In terms of methodology, this study of runaway production has been constructed as a critical media history, meaning that my goal has been not only to create a detailed chronology of the issue, but also to critically analyze its historical development and function within various sectors of the affected media industries. In this book, runaway production has been treated as a cultural artifact through which dominant ideologies have been alternately negotiated, challenged, and reinforced, including the primacy of Western media industries over processes of cultural production, the so-called natural progression of the global free trade of cultural products, and the degeneracy and ineffectuality of trade unionism. Several industry and government archives were consulted, including the special collections libraries at the Academy of Motion Picture Arts and Sciences, UCLA, and the University of Southern California, the film industry archives at the Wisconsin Historical Society in Madison, and the California State Archives in Sacramento. Through these archives, an extensive catalogue of over two thousand primary source documents was compiled, including popular and trade press articles, government documents, and various organizational and production-related materials.

CHAPTER SYNOPSIS

The chapters in this book have been organized around the major conceptual shifts that emerged in the history of runaway production. Chapter 1 describes the introduction of the issue of runaway production in the late 1940s by Hollywood trade unions protesting the staging of U.S.-backed "frozen funds" productions in Europe. While Hollywood's studio owners and film producers argued that these productions were an extension of the democratic mission of the Marshall Plan to stabilize European economies, Hollywood's "below-the-line" production labor countered that the outsourced productions were a form of "un-Americanism." It is argued that the debates over runaway production in the 1940s and 1950s portended the decreasing power and mobility of below-the-line labor within the newly developing International Division of

Cultural Labor, while at the same time showcasing the increasing power and mobility of Hollywood's ownership class, whose global neoliberal agenda was more closely aligned with the ideologies of free trade and global democracy dominant in postwar Washington.

Chapter 2 follows the discourse of runaway production into the 1960s, when themes of runaway free trade and runaway industry extravagance served as the primary organizing constructs. During this period, Hollywood labor argued that producers were running away from organized labor in search of cheaper alternatives abroad, particularly in the case of labor-intensive blockbuster productions like *Cleopatra* (1963) that were becoming the cornerstone of the industry. Labor also complained that "runaway" actors and directors who insisted on living abroad for tax purposes were driving productions out of Hollywood. It is at this juncture that so-called runaway directors and producers argued for recognition of a distinction between economic and creative runaways—productions staged abroad for location authenticity, and not cost savings. The counterargument was also made that the need to pursue new markets for Hollywood films abroad was vitally important to the growth and stability of the home industry, and trumped any runaway complaints of Hollywood's trade labor. The growing tensions between Hollywood's above- and below-the-line labor classes over runaway production are argued to reflect Massey's (1984) theory of global labor power geometry, in which certain privileged groups not only exercise more mobility within an international division of labor, but also more control over the flow of capital and investment within the system. This power differential extends to the construction of "authentic" images within the global mediascape (Appadurai, 1996).

Chapter 3 examines the distinctive shift in runaway production debates towards domestic competition in the 1970s and 1980s. Several states not previously known for their affiliation with film and television production began setting up their own state film commissions and aggressively courting the industry during this time, including Georgia, Florida, and Texas. As Hollywood stalwarts like Dino de Laurentiis and Disney Studios began investing more heavily in production facilities in other states, Hollywood's production labor increasingly framed the discourse of runaway production around right-to-work laws and other state incentives that they perceived to be anti-competitive. The growing emphasis on domestic and regional production competition in the 1970s and 1980s is argued to demonstrate how processes of globalization tend to function through multiple modes of organization, including municipal, local, and international contexts (Pieterse, 2004). It is also argued that the subject of domestic runaway production played into a "divide and conquer" strategy employed by Hollywood's studios and producers who used regional competition to isolate and weaken the bargaining power of organized production labor in the United States. (Christopherson, 2005). Also discussed in this chapter is the negotiation of a "runaway clause" by Hollywood's animation guild in an effort to stem the outsourcing of labor-intensive "ink and paint" work overseas. Animation labor's runaway story is one that ultimately hinges on the use of new digital communication technologies to manage the global distribution of animation work—a scenario that reflects the function of the "technoscape" in processes of globalization.

In the fourth and final chapter, the primary focus is on Canadian runaway production. However, given the more substantial academic literature on the development of Canada's industry in the 1990s and 2000s, the discussion instead centers on the counter-discourse to runaway production offered up by Canadian labor. Since the 1980s, Hollywood producers and directors began establishing a production infrastructure in Canada, particularly Toronto and Vancouver, driven by a favorable currency exchange rate as well as regional and national industry subsidies. Much to the dismay of Hollywood production labor, Vancouver is now the third-largest production center in North America, with blockbuster movies like *Fantastic Four* (2005), *Juno* (2007), *50 Shades of Grey* (2015), and *Tomorrowland* (2015) filmed in whole or in part in the city that has earned the nickname Hollywood North. On one level, the discursive battle between Hollywood and Canadian labor represents a continuation of the regionalization of labor competition in the New International Division of Cultural Labor (NICL). It also is argued that governmentality, or the instrumental use of national and cultural identity by governments in the service of transnational industries, has become a guiding logic in the debates over runaway Canadian subsidies in the 1990s and 2000s (Bennett, 1992).

NOTE

1. In addition to motion picture and television programs, the U.S. International Trade Commission also includes recorded music, music videos, and recorded video tapes and disks in the category of "audiovisual services." (U.S. International Trade Commission, 2001, pp. 6–10).

Chapter One

Hollywood at the Crossroads

Runaway Film Production and the Postwar Film Industry[1]

The story of runaway production begins in postwar Hollywood, when below-the-line studio labor anxiously awaited the return to prewar production levels. But in this postwar period, four major events occurred that would forever change the way Hollywood did business: The Paramount Decision, the mass adoption of television around 1948, the Anglo-American Film Pact of 1950, and the House Un-American Activities Committee hearings in Hollywood in 1947 and 1951. Each of these events, in their own way, served as an incentive for Hollywood producers to take more of their productions abroad—to make up for lost exhibition revenues, to expand to new markets, to recoup "frozen" exhibition funds from recovering European nations, and to flee political persecution. Perhaps not surprisingly, Hollywood's below-the-line labor leaders began using the phrase "runaway production" during this time, describing film productions produced by Hollywood studios but filmed overseas. In this original context, runaway production is argued to represent the fear and frustration of a labor community being left behind by a globalizing industry. But more specifically, I argue that runaway production is a reaction to the de-territorialization and mobilization of the Hollywood production process. The Hollywood studio was no longer a sacred space to produce movies, and the workers in those studios were no longer the exclusive labor force for the Hollywood motion picture industry. Runaway production was therefore a response to the establishment of the New International Division of Cultural Labor (NICL), in which the film production process and its labor force could be distributed around the world in ways that best served the political and economic needs and obligations of the Hollywood industry.

The postwar political and economic recovery of Europe and the development of the Cold War were, of course, intricately intertwined. And as such, these events and their related discourses frequently appeared side-by-side in the early history of runaway film production. Together, they paint a compelling picture of the dramatic shift toward global markets made by the Hollywood film industry (along with many other industries) following the war. Yet, as Malcolm Waters (2001) has argued, globalization is more than a shift toward globalized modes of production, but is also "a social process in which the constraints of geography on economic, political, social and cultural arrangements recede, in which people become increasingly aware that they are receding and in which people act accordingly" (p. 5). The discourse of runaway film production in the postwar era arguably reflects the increasing awareness among Hollywood labor of their receding role within a globalizing film industry, and their need to "act accordingly" and fight to maintain a significant position within the New International Division of Cultural Labor.

SETTING THE STAGE FOR THE RUNAWAY DEBATES

Though the discourse of runaway production would bring attention to the practice of Hollywood production overseas in the late 1940s, it by no means signaled the beginning of such practices. On the contrary, Hollywood's majors had actively pursued both distribution and production opportunities in Europe for most of the 1920s and 1930s. During these decades, foreign markets brought in approximately 35 percent of Hollywood's exhibition revenues, with English-speaking countries, namely Great Britain, representing 50 percent of revenues earned outside the United States and Canada (Balio, 1996, p. 32; Thompson, 1985). With such significant earnings on the line, Hollywood film interests looked for ways to both sustain and perhaps expand European markets.

But Hollywood's inroads in the European market were dramatically curtailed as World War II approached. In 1929, Hollywood had distributed over 200 films to the German market. By 1932, the number of films dropped to fifty, and by 1936, Germany was no longer accepting film imports from the United States (Balio, 1996, p. 35). It was a similar story in Italy and Spain. The British market, a lucrative distribution and trade outlet for the Hollywood majors, also fell off the distribution charts as theaters were boarded up with the beginning of Nazi bombing raids in 1939.

Back at home, the Hollywood production industry had managed to survive the Great Depression relatively unscathed. Though movie attendance had taken a hit in 1932, the numbers began to rebound by the following year, jumping from an average weekly attendance of 60 million in 1933 to 88 million by 1936 (Balio, 1996, p. 30). Despite the relative economic stability of the Hollywood film industry, the 1930s and 1940s proved to be a tumultuous time for Hollywood production labor. The film industry's largest trade union, the International Alliance of Theatrical and Stage Employes (IATSE), had engaged in a protracted, and sometimes violent, battle with the Conference of Studio Unions (CSU) for jurisdiction over Hollywood's studios. From these events emerged some of the key voices within the earliest debates over runaway film production in Hollywood. And it is also through these events that the issue of runaway film production became inextricably linked with other important political agendas in Hollywood at the time, namely the campaign against Communist infiltration of the industry at home and abroad.

Even before foreign competition appeared on the radar of Hollywood's labor unions, turmoil within their unions had set the organizations off kilter. In 1937, thirty-seven set decorators left IATSE to form their own representative labor group, the Society of Motion Picture Interior Decorators (SMPID). They became affiliated with the Conference of Studio Unions in 1944—a group with suspected communist leanings—after a failed attempt to certify their contract with the National Labor Relations Board (NLRB). IASTE leadership disputed the set decorators' affiliation with the CSU, as well as the legitimacy of their contract, arguing that some of the set decorators were still members of Hollywood's IA Local 44. IATSE's strategy ultimately worked: SMPID's contract negotiations stalled for several months, forcing the CSU into a protracted strike that lead to the notorious Black Friday riots outside Warner Brothers studios on October 5, 1945 (Horne, 2001).

Disturbed by the violent tactics of the CSU and eager to restore order to the industry, IATSE international president Richard Walsh went in search of a union steward who could restore order to Hollywood's IA local and reinstate its jurisdiction over wayward members. Walsh found that person in Roy M. Brewer, a labor leader from Oklahoma who had made a name for himself organizing his state's film projectionists at the age of 16 and becoming the youngest president of Oklahoma's AFL at age 23 (King, 1953). Brewer's first order of business as head of Hollywood's IATSE local was to begin a relentless smear campaign against the CSU and its leader Herb Sorrell. Sorrell's reputation as a labor leader was already in tatters after the Black Friday incident, having been found guilty of inciting a riot and sent to jail for a short time, though he was later acquitted on all charges. Brewer marked Sorrell as part of a communist conspiracy to infiltrate Hollywood labor organizations to gain access to the motion picture industry, which could then be used as a covert propaganda tool by the "Reds." By 1948, Brewer's strategy had effectively dismantled the CSU along with Herb Sorrell's credibility as a labor leader. Producers afraid of being associated with a known or suspected communist organization quickly fell in support of IATSE's agenda, creating untenable working conditions for CSU members in their studios, and forcing the organization into yet another strike that dealt the final blow to their already depleted coffers. Roy Brewer had accomplished what he'd been hired to do: put down the CSU insurrection and restore the IATSE's jurisdictional dominance within Hollywood's studio system. With the confidence of Hollywood's labor community behind him, Brewer was ready to take on another looming threat—the increasingly common practice of making Hollywood films abroad.

In the years following the CSU strikes, Brewer became integrally involved in two powerful union coalitions in Hollywood: The Motion Picture Industry Council (MPIC) and the Hollywood AFL Film Council. It is through these organizations that Brewer campaigned against foreign production practices and helped forge the discourse of runaway film production. Organized in 1947, the Hollywood AFL Film Council was a group comprised of representatives from nearly all of Hollywood's film industry unions. The Council boasted representation of over 25,000 organized workers in the Hollywood film industry, including members of the Screen Actors and Screen Extras Guilds, the Teamsters, Studio Janitors, and the IATSE. (Brewer, 1948). In an American Federation of Labor newsletter, Brewer described the purpose of the Council as an attempt to unite union laborers affiliated with the AFL within the motion picture industry. In truth, it had only been three years since the violent CSU strike activity at Warner Bros. Most within the Hollywood film industry understood the establishment of the Council to be an attempt to portray stability and peace in the industry, not only among the workers, but between the labor organizations and the producers as well. With the House Un-American Activities Committee turning its eye toward Hollywood at precisely this time, it is also likely that the AFL Film Council was meant to represent a united, anticommunist front.

The MPIC was formed on the heels of the AFL Film Council in 1948. The MPIC was similarly part of an industry-wide effort to repair relations between Hollywood's producers and labor organizations, and between the labor organizations themselves, in the aftermath of the IATSE-CSU confrontation. With more of a focus on representing the film industry's above-the-line labor and management class, the MPIC was comprised of a mix of ten major Hollywood organizations, including the Screen Writers' Guild, the Screen Actors Guild, the Society of Motion Picture Art Directors, the Motion Picture Producers Association, the Screen Directors' Guild, Independent Office Workers, and the AFL Film Council (Arthur, 1949). One of the MPIC's primary functions was as an industry liaison in matters pertaining to inter- and intra-industry policy development, including consultation on censorship rules and international film trade policies (Academy of Motion Picture Arts and Sciences, 2007). The Motion Picture Association of America (MPAA) was the central agent involved in the direct negotiation of such matters, particularly regarding international trade policy development. But it was widely accepted that the MPAA represented the voice of the "majors" and their corporate interests, and not necessarily the interests of those more directly involved in the production process. As such, the MPIC was meant to provide a consulting body for the production sector of the industry that functioned separately from the MPAA, but that could also work in conjunction with the MPAA when policy issues arose that had the potential to impact production. One such issue surfaced in 1950, concerning British "frozen funds" production and the negotiation of the Anglo-American Film Pact by the MPAA.

POSTWAR "FROZEN FUNDS" AND OVERSEAS PRODUCTION

Film production and exhibition across Europe had ground to a near-standstill during World War II. Many theaters in England and across Europe had been forced to close due to economic or political constraints, and in many cases, both. Before the war, Hollywood studios were earning roughly 30 percent of their exhibition revenues from foreign markets (Guback, 1976, p. 394). Naturally, the Hollywood studios were eager to pick up where they had left off, with stockpiles of films ready for export to postwar Europe. But the European economy had changed drastically because of the war, with many countries left in dire financial straits. Despite efforts to stabilize the currency imbalances among European nations impacted by the war, mainly through the Bretton Woods Agreement of 1944, many still found themselves strapped for cash and precipitously close to national bankruptcy.

England instituted several economic measures to try to stem the flow of cash from their already-depleted coffers, including a precipitous 75 percent import tax on American films, as well as a $17 million cap on exportable U.S. film exhibition revenues; proceeds exceeding the $17 million mark were conditionally "frozen" by the British government (p. 397). U.S. film interests and their Congressional counterparts were outraged by the measures, and immediately organized an embargo on the export of U.S. films to England. British theater owners reacted with anger and panic, as they relied on American films to fill approximately 80 percent of their screens: without American films, they argued, their already war-crippled industry would crumble (IATSE, 1948, pp. 225–26).

The standoff between Hollywood and the British government came to a head in March 1948, at which point Eric Johnston was sent to the UK to negotiate a compromise. Harold Wilson, president of the British Board of Trade who would become prime minister in 1964, met with Johnston for ten days before reaching a final settlement on March 11. The newly-drafted Anglo

American Film Pact lifted the import tax on American films but maintained the $17 million cap on exportable revenues, with two important concessions: U.S. film interests could access frozen funds by reinvesting the revenues in the UK, and specifically the British film industry, or by purchasing the rights to distribute British films in the United States (Political and Economic Planning, 1952, p. 101; *Hansard* 06 April 1948 col 1095–96). The Pact was limited to four years, at which point the terms could be renegotiated. By some estimates, the United States earned $50–70 million a year in film exhibition returns in Great Britain; the Film Pact obligated Hollywood majors to reinvest approximately two-thirds of these earnings in the British economy. It was a compromise Johnston and the studio execs were willing to live with, but one that Hollywood labor bitterly resented.

Labor leaders and members of Hollywood's production community were apprehensive about the Anglo-American Agreement, and worried about its impact on domestic production work. But at least initially, Hollywood labor was sympathetic to the economic plight of their wartime ally. At the 1948 biannual convention of the IATSE, Tom O'Brien, MP and general secretary of the U.K.'s National Association of Theatrical and Kine Employees (NATTKE),[2] addressed the delegation at the behest of IATSE international president Richard Walsh. The official proceedings from the convention described a "warm and sincere" reception from the crowd, followed by a "heartfelt address" by O'Brien (IATSE, 1948, p. 223). The general tone of his speech was conciliatory, stating that the 75 percent import tax was not intended to be "anti-American" or "anti-Hollywood." The British had been forced to cut back on food imports and other necessities, and considering such cutbacks, the tens of millions paid out annually for Hollywood film exhibitions could no longer be justified without imposing an import tax (p. 225). O'Brien applauded the MPAA's Eric Johnston for his efforts in negotiating the Anglo-American Agreement, arguing that many in Parliament, including himself, had also been working to convince England's Board of Trade to retract the import tax. In the end, he encouraged continued cooperation between the British and American film industries, not only for the mutual betterment of each country's economy, but also in the interest of a mutual commitment to fight totalitarianism around the world:

> The only people who will benefit by the collapse of the American and British film industries will be those who want to ruin them in order to control them for Un-American and Un-British political ends. The stage and the films, once in the hands of the enemies of Democracy, would make the destruction of Democracy the more certain. (pp. 228–29)

The unity and goodwill prescribed in O'Brien's speech seems only to have lasted a few short months. By February 1949, IATSE and the Hollywood AFL Film Council were engaged in a full-bore lobbying effort—through the press as well as political channels—against frozen funds "runaway" production in England.

Six months after IATSE's convention, the Hollywood AFL Film Council formed a special subcommittee on foreign production. Headed by John Lehners, business agent of the Hollywood Editors Guild, the committee was to investigate the practice of American companies using frozen funds to shoot films in places like England and Italy, and to explore ways of discouraging the practice (AFL Council to ask, 1949). The Council pressured Hollywood producers to find a more equitable solution to the frozen funds problem, and threatened to lobby for a government ban on the exhibition of foreign runaway films in the United States if none was offered (Brady, 1949). On March 7, 1949, John Lehners and Roy Brewer of the AFL Film Council met with Eric Johnston and Y. Frank Freeman of the MPPA at the Beverly Hills Hotel to work out a compromise. According to the *Los Angeles Times*, "It was agreed unanimously that one of the principal causes of unemployment in Hollywood studios [was] the freezing in foreign countries of income earned by their American films" (Unions to Help Film Producers, 1949, p. A1). It was also agreed that the MPAA, AFL Film Council, and the Producers Association would work together to find alternative investments, beyond foreign movie production, for accessing frozen funds in Europe.

A few weeks later, Roy Brewer and SAG representative Kenneth Thomson went to Washington D.C. to directly solicit Congressional support for counter-restrictions on British film imports. The first to join their cause was Senator William F. Knowland, a Republican from California with an interest in foreign policy and the fight against Communism overseas. He described British screen quotas on American films as "rank discrimination" (Action Sought against British, 1949, p. A8) and accused the British government of constructing "economic iron curtains" (Arthur, 1949, p. 4) through their frozen funds policies. In April 1949, members of the Motion Picture Industry Council, which included Roy Brewer and Richard Walsh of IATSE, Kenneth Thomson of the Screen Writers' Guild, and Ronald Reagan, president of the Screen Actors Guild, were sent to meet with President Truman to discuss the problem of frozen funds policies in Europe, and the economically damaging trend of "runaway" film production. Truman was described as having given the group his "sympathetic attention" on the matter (p. 3). The next week they met with Secretary of State Dean Acheson, urging the State Department to hold the British government to Article IV of the General Agreement on Tariffs and Trades (GATT) regarding the "limitation, liberalization or elimination" of screen quotas (Arthur, 1949, p. 1; Film Council asks U.S. Act on British Quotas, 1949, p. A2). In a discussion draft of the proposal put before the State Department, Art Arthur of the MPIC went on to express his deep misgivings with the British situation, suggesting intentions for their film quota policies beyond economic recovery. Though Arthur was not willing to go as far as Senator Knowland in suggesting that British film quotas were part of a communist conspiracy, his comments effectively labeled the policies as anti-competitive and anti-Capitalist—a critique that would have carried greater significance during the Cold War. There's no evidence to suggest that the State Department engaged in a serious investigation of the Anglo-American Film Pact or the threat of runaway production following the meetings with the AFL Film Council and MPIC. Instead, film industry labor leaders put their faith in Eric Johnston of the MPAA to address their concerns in the renegotiation of the Anglo-American Agreement in 1950.

Though the original Anglo-American Film Pact called for a renegotiation of terms after four years, all parties were called back to the table in 1950 after only two years. Economic conditions in the United Kingdom had improved more quickly than anticipated, giving the Hollywood majors hope that they could finally negotiate the end of frozen funds restrictions. In the months leading up to the talks, the Hollywood unions continued to put pressure on producers to reduce foreign motion picture production—almost exclusively referred to as "runaway production" by this point—while seeking their own political solutions, including a ban on British film imports (Hollywood Labor Won't, 1950). Once again, Eric Johnston was put in the position of mollifying the unions in the lead up to the new Film Pact negotiations. In a meeting with the AFL Film Council in April 1950, Johnston argued that frozen funds policies resulted in no more than a dozen or so overseas film productions every year—a small price to pay for the long-term health of the Hollywood motion picture industry (Spiro, 1950). He assured the Council members that most films produced by Hollywood studios, close to 400 in 1949, were made in the "Western Hemisphere." He also explained that most frozen funds investments overseas were in industries other than motion picture production, including shipbuilding in France and textiles in Italy (Spiro, 1950, p. X5). Roy Brewer, chairman of the AFL Film Council, temporarily conceded Johnston's point in the trade press following their meeting. But overall, the Council was unconvinced that Hollywood labor would benefit from foreign production.

Unemployment in Hollywood had climbed precipitously following the first Anglo-American Film Pact. In 1946, the Hollywood motion picture industry employed 24,000 people; in 1950, two years after the first Pact took effect, that number was down to 13,000 (Bernstein, 1957, p. 31). The cause-effect relationship between the two circumstances was, of course, dubious. Many industry changes, not the least of which being competition from television, were scaling down the number of films produced annually by the major studios (Balio, 1976). But the rallying cry against foreign runaway production had momentum with labor supporters, aligning with the protectionist discourse of Cold War America. And not coincidently, several members of the AFL Film Council, including Ronald Reagan and Roy Brewer, were cooperating with the controversial House Un-American Activities Committee investigations of the Hollywood industry around the same time as the Film Pact negotiations.

The new round of Anglo American Film Pact talks was set to begin May 15, 1950 in Dublin—a location described as "neutral territory" for discussions of an issue that almost exclusively involved the United States and England (IATSE, 1950, p. 74). Eric Johnston was joined by James A. Mulvey of Samuel Goldwyn Productions, who had also participated in negotiations of the first agreement in 1948. A third member of the U.S. negotiating team was Ellis G. Arnall of the Society of Independent Motion Picture Producers (SIMPP). Arnall served as governor of Georgia from 1943 to 1947, after which he was recruited by the SIMPP to help break up the monopoly of the Hollywood majors. The SIMPP had filed the original anti-trust suit that led to the Supreme Court's Paramount Decision in 1948, forcing the Hollywood majors to relinquish control of their theater chains and allowing independents to compete for U.S. screen space on a level playing field. But independent producers from the United States, like the Hollywood majors, were also heavily invested in production and distribution overseas, and were united in their efforts to gain more access to frozen funds in the UK.

A week before leaving for Dublin, Arnall met with the Hollywood AFL Film Council to assure its members that a "firm stance" would be taken with the British in resolving the frozen funds issue (Hollywood Labor Won't Back Down, 1950). As reported in *Variety*, Arnall promised the labor leaders that no deals would be made that continued to support the *quid pro quo*, "frozen funds for foreign production" policy. Arnall and the other U.S. negotiators anticipated a "knockdown dragout session with the British," as the latter were expected to argue for a decrease in exportable exhibition revenues, and a continuation of Hollywood investments in the British film industry and beyond (p. 22).

Even though Hollywood's old-guard producers were trying to get out from under the Anglo-American Film Agreement, they chafed at the idea of Hollywood's unions labeling frozen funds foreign productions as runaway productions. In a *Variety* editorial written by Arthur Hornblow, Jr., an MGM producer known for his work on *Gaslight* (1944) and *Asphalt Jungle* (1950), he advised the unions to wake up to the fact that film production was no longer just a Hollywood industry, but an increasingly global one. And like Johnston before him, he insisted that the health of the Hollywood industry was integrally dependent on the health of foreign markets and production: "We're all going to travel a great deal more than we've done in the past. . . . Hollywood would fall upon its worst days if income from overseas sources were restricted" (Hornblow Accents Inevitability, 1950, p. 2).

As the Anglo-American renegotiations began in mid May, Eric Johnston emphasized the fact that production levels had fallen off not only in Hollywood, but internationally, in part due to war recovery. Under the circumstances, it was unrealistic for the British to expect American producers to spend down all of the $50,000,000 frozen in the UK. Rather, The British Board of Trade needed to provide new and more flexible provisions (U.S. Leaders in London, 1950). The deadline for renewal of the 1948 agreement was June 11, but progress in the initial talks between Johnston and British Board president Harold Wilson was slow.

As expected, the Brits proposed to decrease the amount of funds that could be exported by the U.S. film industry annually, as well as the percentage that could be accessed through the production of American films on British soil. A new "incentive" provision was put on the table, which offered American producers access to fifty cents on the dollar for monies invested in the making of British "quota" films. films meant to fulfill the 40 percent British exhibitionary quota set for British movie theaters (Gains Small for British Film Talks, 1950). The British film quota system was put into place in the 1920s in response to the overwhelming dominance of U.S. films in British theaters. Hollywood films occupied around 95 percent of theater offerings in 1925, earning roughly one-third of Hollywood's foreign box office revenues (Balio, 1996, p. 390). This alarming trend precipitated the passing of the British Films Act of 1927, instituting a graduated screen quota system in which British-made films were intended to increase in theater representation in the UK from 5 percent to 20 percent over ten years. The unanticipated result was a decline in the quality of British films, as American producers backed the production of fast and cheap British "quota quickies" to meet the requirements of the law, while also perhaps bolstering the demand for superior quality Hollywood films (Greenwald, 1952).

To correct the market, a second Films Act was passed in 1938 that lowered the British screen quota to 12.5 percent with a graduated increase to 25 percent by 1947. The second Act also created a minimum budget requirement to discourage the making of B-grade British quota films. But in 1950, the British film industry was still struggling to meet their national screen quotas, and the frozen funds situation with Hollywood seemed like a perfect opportunity to enlist the help of Hollywood in meeting that quota, even if it meant compromising on the British-ness of the films produced. Johnston and the American film interests he represented were adamant that the British economy had experienced substantial recovery since the 1948 Agreement and that the goal should be to ween the British industry from the practice of frozen funds production rather than increase restrictions on revenue access. The American negotiators also understood that the stakes were much higher than their immediate dialogue with the British; they anticipated a domino effect among countries such as Italy and New Zealand who would follow suit in renegotiating their own frozen funds policies.

Union leaders were startled by the possibility of an epidemic of "frozen funds" runaway productions spreading across Europe. Dick Walsh, the IATSE's international president, had been asked to meet with Eric Johnston in Dublin during the Anglo-American talks to provide his opinions on deals on the table. Upon his return, Walsh presented his experience in Ireland as a cautionary tale to IATSE convention delegates. He described how Eric Johnston was peppered with questions about when the American film industry would start staging productions in Ireland. Like an infectious disease, Walsh expressed concern that frozen funds productions could spread to other European countries, to which he concluded, "And if they start multiplying the British situation, then we really will feel it—badly—in Hollywood" (IATSE, 1950, p. 74). However, after meeting with British labor leaders in Europe, Walsh admitted feeling some sympathy for their industry: the percentage of unemployment among British studio employment was much higher than in Hollywood. He even admitted that American productions in England were "a great help to them, more than they are a loss to us" (p. 74). But ultimately he disagreed with their "so-called incentive program":

> Americans do not take kindly to coercion. When governments start telling producers where to make pictures, then I believe that labor—even at the risk of intruding upon the rights of free enterprise—may be warranted in using its power to help call a halt. (p. 74)

In retrospect, Walsh's comments were both prophetic and naïve: prophetic in their detection of the growing importance—and danger—of multinational state and corporate collusion in matters of media trade and production, and naïve in their assumption that labor had agency within such a multinational system. The ethos of global capitalism and the New International Division of Cultural Labor was already deeply embedded among Hollywood's ownership class, and Eric Johnston was its most important emissary. In his regular address to the IA delegates, Johnston seemed to have had the good sense not to dwell on the Anglo-American talks and their role in instituting an international division of film labor. Rather, he spoke more generally of the role of the American motion picture industry and its films as harbingers of goodwill and democracy around the world—an important function during the uncertain days of the Cold War (p. 216).

Johnston's speech was well-received by the IATSE delegates, though in many ways his arguments contradicted the primary goal of the union—to end runaway foreign production. Instead, Johnston's justifications for overseas production exemplified the increasing political momentum towards "corporate transculturalism" (Kraidy, 2005), in which capitalism and democracy are conflated in order to rationalize global economic trailblazing. By Johnston's logic, the Hollywood film industry was not exporting jobs—it was exporting democracy. And as a global emissary of democratic ideals, it was not only anticipated, but *expected* that the Hollywood film industry would collaborate with overseas governments and production communities with questionable political and economic affiliations. This was perhaps Johnston anticipating an imminent frozen funds production deal with Italy, which would surely produce protests from fervent anticommunist Hollywood labor leaders such as Roy Brewer. As such, Johnston's speech also provides a textbook example of the use of anticommunist ideology as a mechanism for mollifying labor while paradoxically justifying U.S. corporate collusion with potentially fascist political and economic interests abroad (Herman & Chomsky, 2002). As framed by Johnston, it would be un-democratic and un-American for Hollywood labor to protest overseas production when the purpose was to spread democratic ideals.

After eight months of negotiation, the second Anglo-American Film Agreement was finally signed on December 5, 1950. Though the new Agreement kept the $17 million annual cap on exportable U.S. film revenues in place, it included several new "incentives" for Americans to claim frozen revenues above and beyond the limit: they could claim 23 percent of the amount invested in the making of British quota films; they could access 50 percent of revenues paid to British distributors for distributing American films on a percentage basis in the Western Hemisphere; and they could claim 50 percent of payments made to British interests for copyrights in the Western Hemisphere. Americans were also given the ability to convert British earnings into the currency of a third country, given the consent of all concerned governments (Political and Economic Planning, 1952, p. 160). Producers viewed the new Agreement as a coup, seeing the British incentives as progress toward an eventual free trade agreement and removal of the revenue cap. Hollywood labor, however, saw the added "incentives" as a ploy for further entrenchment of American producers in overseas film production and further divestment from the Hollywood production community.

Though disappointed with the outcome of the second Anglo-American Agreement, Hollywood labor appeared to reevaluate and refresh their approach to the issue of runaway film production rather than abandon the cause. Their attempts to garner sympathy for unemployed Hollywood film workers had fallen flat. And yet producers had managed to win support for the Anglo-American Agreement and foreign production practices through the ideologies of anticommunism and corporate transculturalism: framing global capitalism as a cure-all for both our allies' economic woes and our enemies' political threats.

But Cold War ideologies could cut both ways. Hollywood labor, and specifically IATSE, had already used the discourse of anticommunism to win back jurisdiction over studios in the 1940s. In the case of runaway film production, labor would have to deconstruct the persona Hollywood producers had created for themselves as democratic reformers, and instead paint them as un-American, fascist collaborators. In a Hollywood left skittish by the House Un-American Activities Committee hearings, it seemed like a promising strategy. But with so much momentum already behind the free trade movement in Hollywood, and so much to gain—politically and economically—if overseas markets were opened permanently to the Hollywood industry, labor was facing an uphill battle.

RUNAWAY UN-AMERICANISM

The potential use of the Hollywood film industry as a communist propaganda tool had been a point of concern for the American anticommunist movement from the very beginning of the Cold War. The film industry unions had been looked upon as the most logical entry-point for communist infiltration of the industry before World War II. But the House Un-American Activities Committee seemed less concerned with communist infiltration of below-the-line labor in the 1950s, especially with one of the most vocal anti-communists in Hollywood at the helm of IATSE and the AFL Film Council—Roy Brewer. Instead, Hollywood's high-profile, above-the-line labor—actors, writers, directors—were the primary targets of investigations of communist influence within the film industry. Screenwriters were under intense scrutiny, drawing accusations that scripts were being "coded" with communist messages (Eckstein, 2004, p. 429).[3]

With suspicion already cast on certain individuals and occupations within the industry, it wasn't much of a stretch for below-the-line labor to connect the ideology of anticommunism with the discourse of runaway film production; as we've seen, this had already begun to occur during the frozen funds production debates. After the negotiation of the second Anglo American Agreement in 1950, however, the unions began to lean more heavily on the

McCarthyist anthem of un-Americanism as the principal underlying motivation for foreign runaway film production. First, labor argued that producers were taking productions overseas to accommodate Hollywood talent "running" from the anti-communist scrutiny of Hollywood; second, they argued that more productions were being staged overseas to accommodate Hollywood elites "running" from their democratic obligation to pay U.S. income taxes via a residency loophole called the 18-month rule; third, they accused producers of running away from American unions and toward cheap, non-union, and possibly communist labor overseas; and finally, labor contended that runaway film producers and TV advertisers were misrepresenting American culture and purposely deceiving American audiences by not disclosing their projects as foreign productions.

With these four instances of runaway un-Americanism in mind, it is argued that Hollywood labor attempted to tap into the anticommunism, pro-democracy "ideoscape" (Appadurai, 1996) as a means for disciplining runaway film producers and directors and reterritorializing their industry—politically and economically—within the United States. As history will show, labor was unsuccessful in using anticommunism to garner public and governmental support for their efforts to stop runaway film production. This may be attributed to labor's diminishing power within the New International Division of Cultural Labor, as well as the increasing power and agency of multinational media corporations to both define and function outside of the ideological constraints of nation-states. (Appadurai, 1996; Miller, et al., 2001)

Runaway Production and the IATSE Convention of 1952

In the years immediately following the second Anglo American Film Agreement, the scope of the runway production debates quickly expanded beyond European frozen funds policies. And in fact, by 1952 Hollywood labor leaders had done an about face, publicly stating that frozen funds production and foreign production for location authenticity (aka creative runaways) were acceptable reasons for filming outside the United States (Spiro, 1952). As such, the IATSE convention in Minneapolis that year proved to be an important venue for redefining the meaning of runaway production. And one major industry development on the minds of conventioneers that year was television.

Though film production was still the primary concern for Hollywood labor in the early 1950s, television production had become an increasingly important sector of their industry. At first, Hollywood labor had been apprehensive about the potential effects of television on their work: movie attendance in the United States had reached an all-time high during the war.[4] But box office revenues began to decline dramatically as the popularity of television increased, with theater revenues falling 23 percent from 1946 to 1956 (Balio, 1976, p. 315). Hollywood labor naturally felt the effects, with employment dropping from 24,000 to 13,000 during the same ten-year period (p. 316). Due to the mass suburbanization of the United States following the war, people were moving out of urban centers and away from the old movie palaces. Television was the perfect medium for this new, spatially dispersed population in need of information and entertainment while remaining in the comfort and privacy of their own homes (Spigel 1992; Williams, 2003). But in the end, television programs were no different than films in that they needed to be made by skilled labor using soundstages, lighting equipment, and many other production elements primarily found in Hollywood at the time. Before long, the increasing demand for television content, including entertainment programming and advertising, was viewed as crucial to Hollywood's postwar recovery.

In the months leading up to the 1952 IATSE convention, union statements concerning foreign production began to include television, and specifically the production of advertisements made abroad but intended for American audiences ("Run-away" Foreign Film Production Irks, 1952). They argued that such production practices were un-American as they were luring away American jobs. What's more, they accused industry producers of being dishonest in their attempt to "sell American products to American workers by means of advertising films that have been made in foreign countries by foreign workers" (Film Council Threatens Boycott, 1952, p. 8). The Council passed a strongly-worded resolution, calling for a boycott by union members of products represented in such foreign-made commercials. Their resolution was followed by a similar document, submitted by nine members of Hollywood's International Sound Technicians Local 695, in which they called for an officially-stated position on the production of American advertising overseas (IATSE, 1952, p. 296).

Herbert Aller, the business agent for the camera operators union and an appointed delegate to the IATSE convention, argued for a resolution to establish a boycott program called "Don't Buy" that would target manufacturers who were "connected with and responsible for the production of motion pictures under such run-away tactics" (p. 297). Participants in the boycott would include members of the American Federation of Labor, the State Labor Federations, and the Central Labor Council of the United States. IATSE President Richard Walsh tabled the amendment pending further review, with concerns that the wording could lead to legal "complications." Similar resolutions denouncing runaway television production were proposed over the next few years: SAG delegates called for a nationwide effort to stop runaway foreign production of television commercials during the California State

Theatrical Federation and New York's State Federation of Labor conventions of 1955 (State Federation Opens, 1955); and in 1956, resolutions against the filming of made-for-TV movies were proposed at the biennial IATSE convention (IATSE, 1956, pp. 320–21).

Discussions of runaway television production would continue to resurface over the next fifty years, particularly regarding the outsourcing of TV animation work. But perhaps due to the impracticality of requiring actors and directors to work abroad on multiple seasons of television shows, and the difficulty of creating television content that could appeal to U.S. audiences and foreign audiences alike (Bielby & Harrington, 2005; Fiske, 1987), incidents of so-called runaway television production remained limited until the 1990s and 2000s, when Canada began to attract many U.S. series.

Eric Johnston was again present at the 1952 convention, and made his "state of the industry" address to the delegates, discussing "the economic present, and the economic future of the motion picture" (IATSE, 1952, p. 178). Johnston wanted to highlight the positive developments in the industry, and chided the "crepe hangers" predicting the demise of Hollywood. Instead, he saw an industry that was still vital, although certainly changing. True, theater attendance was down, and some theaters were even closing. But new theaters were also being built and new exhibition technologies were being developed and implemented. Johnston pointed to the success of the drive-in as evidence of the changing and growing industry, with drive-ins accounting for 20 percent of gross exhibition revenues in 1952, and the number of facilities growing from 155 in 1946 to 4000 just six years later (p. 180).

But Johnston also admitted there would be challenges for the U.S. film industry in the years to come: the rising costs of production, for which he recommended more production "efficiency" rather than the lowering of wages or the increasing of hours worked for the same pay; higher exhibition taxes; the changing social dynamics created by the postwar baby boom, including younger marriages and more household obligations; and of course the growing popularity of television, which he mentioned only very briefly. But Johnston tried to put those challenges in historical perspective by reminding the delegates of past challenges that were overcome by the industry: the shift from silent films to talkies; the rise of radio; and the great depression. In the end, Johnston declared that the industry had entered the "electronic age," and credited technological innovation with the continuing survival of the industry, including the development of 3D and new technologies for recording sound and color (p. 182). In his typically effusive fashion, Eric Johnston ended his speech on a rousing note. Though he acknowledged the years ahead would be difficult, he insisted, "There are mountains of misunderstandings that must be cut through. There are swamps of prejudice that must be filled.

But the idea of tackling these problems, to me, is extremely exhilarating" (p. 183). Johnston's speech provides important insight into the outlook of Hollywood's ownership and management class in the early 1950s, particularly his emphasis on the importance of technology to the progress of the U.S. film industry. Schiller (2000) and Appadurai (1996), among others, have argued the central role of technology, and specifically global telecommunications networks, to the development of global culture industries like TV and film production. Therefore, it is not surprising, even at this early juncture in the "electronic age," to see Johnston pushing for technological solutions to the film industry's labor and production problems—solutions that would ultimately serve the neoliberal agenda of producers and owners, but not the economic protectionist agenda of Hollywood labor.

Johnston's speech had a political message as well. One of the "swamps of prejudice" he referred to was already festering and threatening to divide Hollywood's film industry and labor as it had in the 1940s: the anti-communist movement left in the wake of the House Committee on Un-American Activities hearings. While Hollywood owners and producers were ready to move on from the issue of anticommunism, the HUAC hearings had provided an opportunity for labor to reinvent and legitimize their campaign against foreign runaway production by tying the issue to the federally mandated fight against un-Americanism in Hollywood's film industry.

Un-Americanism and the 18-Month Tax Rule

Runaway film production had found some legitimacy as a discursive critique of foreign policy. But with the issue of frozen funds production essentially resolved, Hollywood labor was in need of a new policy reform initiative, and they found it in an income tax loophole called the "18-month tax rule." Hollywood labor groups, including the AFL Film Council, contended that actors and other above-the-line labor were moving overseas for extended periods of time to qualify for a U.S. income tax exemption, and in the process, taking production work with them. Once this new narrative was integrated with the potent discourse of un-Americanism, Hollywood labor's campaign against the 18-month tax rule was destined to be one of their most successful anti-runaway production efforts.

Hollywood's below-the-line labor leaders were instrumental to the HUAC hearings and their mission to rout communism from the U.S. film industry: Roy Brewer, Ronald Reagan, and other key labor figures served as high profile "friendly" witnesses for both the 1947 and 1951 committee hearings. Brewer was also labeled an architect and enforcer of Hollywood's infamous blacklist—a distinction that earned him the nickname "strawboss for the purge" (Balio, 1976, p. 425). By revoking IATSE certification from films involving people from his list of supposed communist sympathizers, Brewer could doom a picture to failure IATSE projectionists were prohibited from handling a film without certification. And in the early 1950s, IATSE projectionists accounted for virtually all commercial theater projectionists in the United States (McLellan, 2006).

A full year after the 1951 HUAC hearings, Brewer and Hollywood's governing labor councils made it clear that they continued to pledge allegiance to the ideals of the Committee. The Motion Picture Industry Council took out a full-page ad in *Variety* declaring their support for the committee and condemning the anti-HUAC group the Citizens' Committee to Preserve American Freedoms (Once and For All, 1952). Just after the 1952 IA convention, the AFL Film Council requested support from the HUAC in creating legislation that would ban the importation of films believed to be made by "Communists or Pro-Communists persons" living abroad (Film Council Asks Ban, 1952). These actors, directors, and producers were accused of denying Hollywood film workers of jobs by "running away" to countries more tolerant, and perhaps even sympathetic, to communist ideals. Italy and Spain were particularly suspicious film locations for Hollywood's anti-runaway contingency, and productions such as *Roman Holiday* were singled out for their collaborations with Italian crews. But Hollywood labor's problems with *Roman Holiday* also extended to its director, William Wyler, who in many ways served as their archetype of the 1950s "runaway" director.

Wyler was one of the most successful and influential directors in Hollywood in the 1950s, with six Oscar nominations and two wins for best director under his belt before starting work on *Roman Holiday* in 1952. Despite his credentials, Wyler was a thorn in the side of Hollywood labor, most notably for the ways he openly defied their anti-communist and anti-runaway film production movements. In the 1940s, Wyler had formed the Committee for the First Amendment along with director John Huston to show his disapproval of HUAC's activities. In the 1950s, he had left the United States to engage in productions in Europe, collaborating not only with suspected communist unions in Italy, but also with blacklisted and exiled writer Dalton Trumbo on *Roman Holiday*, still working under a pseudonym at the time. Labor also suspected that Wyler had extended his stay in Europe to take advantage of the 18-month income tax exemption rule, which had the effect of drawing production work overseas and away from Hollywood to accommodate him.

In January 1953, the AFL Film Council and MPIC ramped up their campaign against the 18-month tax rule. Their first move was to identify allies in their fight against the "tax cure," starting with a plea for allegiance from the Screen Producers' Guild (SPG). The SPG's president, Sol Seigel, viewed the runaway problem as "out of their jurisdiction," however, and referred Brewer and his cohort to the Association of Motion Picture Producers (AMPP) instead (Siegel Brands IA Beef, 1953). Until an agreement was met with the producers' organization, the AFL Council barred its members from accepting foreign production work, with exceptions for films requiring location shooting or for travel required under the terms of talent contracts (AFL Stiffens Attitude, 1953).

The AFL Film Council met with the AMPP in late January to discuss foreign production practices, and to create some standardized system regarding labor on foreign production that would both suit the needs of producers and employ as many Hollywood union workers as possible (MPIC to Hear Report, 1953). The general reaction from Hollywood producers following the meetings was hostile indignation. Gunter Lessing of the Society of Independent Motion Picture Producers (SIMPP) railed against industry-wide enforcement of any agreement made between the MPIC, the AFL Film Council, and the AMPP:

> No one has the right to speak for the whole industry. We will not be bound by whatever agreement is reached by anyone else. What we do is our own business, as long as it is based on good morals, betterment of production, appropriate economy and the welfare of not just the company or the union but of everyone directly or indirectly concerned. (Gunther Lessing lashes "dictatorial" American Legion, 1953, p. 11)

Lessing saw matters of production, including location choice, as solely the domain of producers and outside the authority and understanding of labor. In a letter to *Variety*, he accused AFL Film Council president Roy Brewer of attempting to "usurp the function of judge, jury and sheriff" and of oversimplifying the otherwise complicated issue of foreign production. Lessing defended the right of producers and directors to decide where a film production should be located, and not production labor. The primary reasons why films ran away, he explained, was due to "sound motives" like accessing frozen funds, seeking more authentic-looking locations and extras, and "cooperation with a government for the purpose of securing import permits for pictures" (Lessing Charges Brewer, 1953, p. 11). Of course, what Lessing and other producers called sound motives for foreign production were precisely the sticking point for labor. It was true that frozen funds production had become generally accepted by labor groups following the Anglo-American Agreements, and location authenticity had always been accepted as a valid reason to shoot abroad. But foreign production for access to authentic extras had not been accepted by the AFL Film Council and the MPIC, particularly since many overseas extras were non-union. Labor also contended that producers' list of motivations for overseas production conveniently left off reasons related to personal gain, including shelter from U.S. income tax through extended foreign residency.

The perceived exploitation of the 18-month tax rule had in fact become a primary motivation for runaway film production by Brewer's assessment. In an adjacent story to Lessing's letter, the AFL Film Council leader listed twenty-one people he claimed were taking advantage of the tax rule, including such beloved Hollywood icons as Humphrey Bogart, Gary Cooper, Kirk Douglas, Gene Kelly, Clark Gable, James Mason, Gregory Peck, Claudette Colbert, Ava Gardner, Lana Turner, John Huston, and William Wyler (Brewer Lists 21 Names, 1953). Lessing countered that it was unrealistic to think that the actions of a few actors could be blamed for the "denial of 'employment for thousands of workers.'" In his opinion, no producer would put themselves in a position of having production decisions dictated to them by the lifestyle preferences of their actors, just as producers weren't about to be dictated to by labor regarding foreign production practices—or so Lessing thought (Lessing Charges Brewer, 1953, p. 11).

The AFL Film Council and MPIC set out to prove Lessing wrong on nearly all counts in the following months. In February, the Councils put pressure on two television sponsors—the Los Angeles Brewery Company and Thrifty Drug—to pull their backing from two shows being filmed outside the United States. *China Smith* had filmed six episodes in Mexico as part of an ongoing storyline in a twenty-six-episode series; an agreement was made with their sponsor, Thrifty Drug, that the six foreign-made episodes would not air, and all future episodes would be made entirely in the United States (AFL Pressures Beer, Drug Companies, 1953; Labor Whips "Runaway" Vipix, 1953; Thrifty Drug Yields to AFL, 1953). Charles Lick of he L.A. Brewery Co. put up resistance to the AFL's request for "cooperation" in discouraging foreign production. However, he eventually gave in to the Council, and did not renew his sponsorship contract with *Foreign Intrigue*, a TV series filmed in Europe (Brewer Charles Lick Protests, 1953).

The AFL Council's aggressive tactics began to raise the ire of some foreign production communities accused of luring Hollywood producers to their countries. In particular, British film labor interests such as the Association of Cinematograph Technicians (ACT) and the Film Industry Employees Council of the UK (a group much like the AFL Film Council in the United States) were fed up with the AFL Film Council's anti-foreign production policies, and were considering a one-day ban on the exhibition of U.S. films in the UK as a sign of protest. The ACT had also sought the support of members of the National Association of Theatrical and Kine Employes (NATKE) in their protest against the American labor groups (Foreign Kickback on AFL Ban, 1953). Before any retaliatory actions were taken, Eric Johnston intervened, managing to both defend U.S. industry production practices overseas and to temporarily placate Brewer and his Council (Johnston, Brewer Reach No Boycott, 1953).

The Hollywood AFL Film Council and the MPIC had launched an aggressive campaign against the 18-month tax rule in Washington. And on April 14, 1953, two bills were introduced to the U.S. Congress proposing amendments to the law (HR 4544; HR 4552). Though the driving forces behind the amendments were the labor councils, support for the proposed amendments was mixed among film unions and guilds. Members of the Screen Actors Guild had been singled out by the Councils as the primary abusers of the 18-month tax law, and ultimately responsible for much runaway production. The Guild leadership challenged these accusations, arguing that among the 208 foreign films imported into the United States in 1952, only 22 had American stars, and only 3 of those actors were eligible for the 18-month tax exemption (Actors Guild Asks Probe, 1953). SAG instead emphasized other possible causes for increases in foreign production, including cheap labor, frozen funds practices, and access to authentic foreign "atmosphere," otherwise known as extras (p. 5). Roy Brewer quickly disputed the Guild's claim in the press, arguing that he could personally name at least thirty-two actors taking advantage of the tax loophole; a noticeable increase from his previous list of twenty-one tax violators, though this time the list never materialized. While still defiant in his position on runaway film production, Brewer's letter to the editor also suggested frustration, and even despondency, as he questioned the long term impact of amending the 18-month tax law on Hollywood's future: "The studios may have started something that won't be easy to stop" (Pryor, 1953, June 7, p. X5). *New York Times* reporter Thomas Pryor added that regardless of the accuracy of Brewer's statements, Hollywood appeared to be entering a "new era" marked by "fewer pictures and faster shooting schedules"; a combination that could only lead to job losses for union film workers (p. X5). In the meantime, the 18-month tax law was a tangible explanation for what might be systemic industry changes, and Hollywood talent living overseas were starting to feel the pressure.

By the end of 1953, the landscape of the campaign against runaway production began to change. In September, Roy Brewer resigned from his position as head of Hollywood's IATSE, taking with him much of labor's zeal for fighting producers on the issue of overseas production (MPIC Revives Anti-red plan, 1953). In a report released in December 1953, the MPIC conceded that while there had been notable increases in foreign production in previous years, the problem was perhaps not as extensive as they had once believed. The report even offered a revised label for foreign made films, called "American-aspect pictures," and defined them as "[a]uthenticated motion pictures produced abroad by American companies; or utilizing recognized American talent; or significantly involving some other American factors" (Pryor, 1953, December 11, p. 42).

With the end of the Brewer era of runaway film production also came a more open derisiveness among producers and directors for the foreign production complaints of labor. Though labor had never strongly argued against location shooting for the sake of authenticity, many directors and producers constructed labor's protests in this way. Some even turned the argument of authenticity back on Hollywood labor to justify their use of European film crews. In a commentary piece titled "The Dissidents Abroad," American director Mitchell Leisen (1954), best known for the films *Death Takes a Holiday* (1934) and *Easy Living* (1937), bemoaned the days when a film featuring Paris had to be shot on "backlot 'French streets' and Stage 12 French Quarters" in Hollywood. Instead, he praised not only the use of authentic settings, but the use of "authentic" crews who knew how to convey their own culture. Up to this point, runaway directors had been very careful to temper their discussions of overseas production with praise and a decided preference for Hollywood crews. Leisen took no such precautions, directly questioning the abilities and authority of Hollywood labor within an increasingly global industry. Directors, producers, and even actors would continue to chide Hollywood's anti-runaway production lobby with the need for "cultural authenticity" and global competitiveness well into the 1960s.

RUNAWAY EXTRAS

Mentions of runaway film production almost completely disappeared from the press over the next few years. Thomas Pryor of the *New York Times* speculated that the growing indifference of the unions to the issue was due to an abundance of television work in Hollywood (Pryor, 1956, September 2). In the mid 1950s, however, a new version on runaway production began to appear that scrutinized union-dodging domestic production practices, particularly in the hiring of film extras—actors without scripted lines, typically used in the backgrounds of scenes, such as a crowd in a baseball stadium.[5] The Screen Extras Guild threatened to walk out of contract talks with movie and television producers over union jurisdiction jumping in Hollywood and San Francisco—taking their productions to locations outside the designated "extra zones" of these cities in order to hire non-union background talent at below-union scale (Pryor, 1956, April 2). Extras' Guild president Richard H. Gordon called this practice runaway production, even though the name had almost exclusively been used to describe overseas production practices up to this point. He argued that increased wages for Hollywood extras would be pointless if producers "are free to ignore AFL-CIO pay scales and conditions by shooting their pictures a sleeper jump away from here" (p. 18). The goal was to extend the Guild's jurisdiction beyond a 300-mile radius of Hollywood so that producers could no longer "run" to outlying counties.

The cost of extras became a recurring theme in defense of "runaway" production in the latter part of the 1950s. With the rise in popularity of large-scale epic films came a demand for literally armies of extras. Producers of such films often argued that it was not only cost prohibitive to hire thousands of extras in Hollywood, but that there simply weren't enough people available to work as extras in Hollywood for such productions. As argued by Ted Richmond, producer for MGM's *Salomon and Sheba* (1959), "Who would make a picture in Hollywood these days if he knew he had to pay nearly $2,000,000 for extras? Metro could not have made 'Ben Hur' in Hollywood either" (Schumach, 1959, p. X7).

In August 1955, the American-backed projects *Daniel Boone* and *Comanche* (1956) were condemned by the AFL Film Council for filming in Mexico for seemingly no other reason than to save money on labor, and specifically extras. The unions were particularly appalled by the runaway production of *Daniel Boone,* as explained by Teamster representative Ralph Clare: "For anything as American as a Daniel Boone film to be produced outside the United States is as un-American as anything" (AFL Film Council Reopens Fight, 1955, p. 9).

As production practices continued to regionalize and globalize over the 1950s, extras became some of the most vulnerable Hollywood labor. And as Hollywood continued to rely more heavily on blockbusters in the following decades, the bargaining power of extras within the New International Division of Cultural Labor would continue to diminish—so much so that by the 2000s, the use of "human" extras in crowd scenes would become something of a novelty with the development of sophisticated computer-generated imagery.

HOLLYWOOD AT A CROSSROADS

As the 1950s were drawing to a close, labor's campaign against runaway film production and un-Americanism appeared to flounder. One of the major problems facing labor was the lack of evidence supporting their contention that overseas production was responsible for increased unemployment in Hollywood. Instead, it had become a game of "he said, he said," with producers countering that overseas production would eventually bring *more* work back to Hollywood by opening new export markets, and therefore generating more revenue that would be used to make more films in the United States. What labor needed was a way to quantify their claims to convince policy makers to side with them in the runaway debate.

In 1957, the AFL Film Council commissioned a study of the economic decline of the U.S. film industry since the end of World War II. Irving Bernstein, a historian and member of UCLA's Institute of Industrial Relation, authored the report *Hollywood at the Crossroads* (1957). Bernstein addressed several key topics, including sales, production, employment, wages, international trade, taxes, and even population trends (p. i). He noted how the economic decline of Hollywood film production was incongruous with the unprecedented growth of the U.S. economy since World War II, and offered seven possible causes for Hollywood's troubles: 1) industry instability created by the breakup of the studio system and the vertical integration of the industry through these companies; 2) the rise of independent production; 3) the phasing out of term contracts for film actors, directors, writers, and producers; 4) the breakdown of the "star system" and the talent drain created by television; 5) the diversification of investments by film companies in both domestic and foreign industries; 6) the rise of the high budget blockbuster; and 7) the loss of traditional executive leadership from the studios (pp. 20–29).

The increase in foreign production and international competition constituted its own chapter in the report. Bernstein described an exchange between MGM head Dore Schary and Eric Johnston of the MPAA regarding the growing Italian industry: "I visited the Cinecitta studios, a thoroughly modern and complete lot, but the only two pictures shooting at the time were David Selznick's 'Farewell to Arms' and Joe Mankiewicz's production of 'The Quiet American.'" Bernstein then asked the rhetorical question, "Where was the Italian industry? And, more important for our purposes, where in the world was the U.S. industry—in Hollywood or in Rome?" (p. 45). Bernstein concluded that the industry had indeed become more global in scope—not just economically, but also cinematically. He explained how the increasing importance of foreign markets for Hollywood film rentals had created a situation where producers couldn't say no when forced to spend frozen revenues overseas—the argument often made by Eric Johnston and other company interests (p. 47). But he also went on to explain that the shift in importance in foreign markets had created a demand for films with more universal appeal; something beyond the American-centric productions of pre-war Hollywood. Subsequently, it was argued that more films were being made abroad to cater to foreign audiences (pp. 47–48). But Bernstein did not agree with the argument that foreign production had little or no impact on Hollywood employment, as often proposed by Eric Johnston and other studio executives. Rather, he stated definitively, "There is no doubt . . . that a substantial volume of employment formerly offered to Hollywood workers has been exported to foreign nations in recent years" (p. 50). Among the motivations he discussed for "American-aspect pictures" to be made abroad, he cited U.S. income tax laws and foreign government subsidies as the most detrimental.

Ultimately, Bernstein's *Hollywood at the Crossroads* did little to advance labor's campaign against runaway film production. Though the report supported a connection between foreign production practices and Hollywood unemployment, it merely muddied the waters by suggesting that many other changes occurring in the industry had also contributed to Hollywood's woes. Bernstein's report also effectively scrubbed the ideological arguments of anti-communism and un-Americanism from the list of explanations behind Hollywood unemployment and runaway film production. Film production—at home and abroad—was a matter of dollars and cents. But more than cost savings, the marketing of American films to the increasingly important global audience had to be taken into greater consideration to bolster foreign exhibition revenues. These conclusions, again, may have been more useful to producers and industry owners. After all, they wanted to treat the production and trade of films on the global market no differently than any other commodity, while labor had mostly constructed their arguments against runaway production on the notion that Hollywood films were a cultural product—that they weren't just any films, they were *American* films produced by an *American* industry. But Bernstein's report may have confirmed what labor feared the most—that the "American-ness" of Hollywood films was becoming less marketable in postwar Europe, and perhaps at home, as well.

Hollywood at the Crossroads seems to have signaled the beginning of the end of the postwar campaign against runaway foreign film production, with key players in the debate making their exit before the decade was over. The Motion Picture Industry Council had been comprised of representatives from both labor and producers' organizations with the intention of creating industry-wide harmony and trust after the violent jurisdictional union battles of the 1940s. But support for an overarching industry council had worn thin as labor and producers had become more divided in their perspectives on foreign production and trade. With little fanfare, the MPIC was disbanded in July 1959; the Hollywood AFL Film Council was left on its own to continue the mission against runaway film production into the 1960s.

CONCLUSION

The formal introduction of the issue of runaway film production in the 1940s and 1950s was in many ways a continuation of already simmering tensions between labor and producers over territorial control of the Hollywood film industry. The established Hollywood unions had barely regained jurisdictional rights over Hollywood's studios in the mid 1940s when the threat of territorial encroachment on their industry was perceived from abroad following the war. Only this time, the "enemy" was not so clearly identified as it had been in the labor disputes with the CSU, or the turf so clearly marked as the Hollywood studios. Rather, the jurisdictional battle that labor found themselves in with producers over postwar runaway film production was waged over the drawing of ideological boundaries as much as spatial boundaries: was the Hollywood film industry a domestic industry with primary obligations to the social, political, and economic agendas of the United States and secondary obligations to foreign markets? Or was Hollywood becoming primarily a global industry, with priorities toward expanding the cultural and economic horizons of the United States? Labor was struggling to maintain Hollywood's identity as a situated place with a unique cultural identity, while producers energetically lobbied to transform the Hollywood industry into a transnational process representative of, but not beholden to, American ideologies—a commodity with extraordinary value to the United States in both political and economic arenas. As Jeremy Packer (2003) has observed, "[T]o be mobile is to be free to govern oneself, across a vast territory, but it is always in accordance with governing in so far as it coincides with 'convenient ends'" (p. 140). The global ambitions of Hollywood's ownership class in the 1940s and 1950s were in perfect concert with the free trade agenda of the postwar United States. And as such, Hollywood's owners and producers had earned a free pass to "govern themselves" on the global free market with little or no interference from federal or state authorities, and certainly with no perceived threat from Hollywood's anti-globalization unions.

Discussions of runaway film production in the 1940s and 1950s also represented deepening frustrations over class divides within the industry. In an increasingly global industry, being above-the-line meant being in control of the location and staging of productions, and subsequently the spatial division of labor as Massey (1984) has described. A film crew was a relatively interchangeable commodity that could be hired on-location, whereas directors and film stars were unique and valuable commodities that had to be accommodated, either by bringing them to the desired location, or bringing the production to them. And as IATSE president Richard Walsh seemed to portend in his comments regarding the Anglo-American Agreement, once such practices of global labor distribution were established, they would be hard to stop. And so, the 1940s and 1950s were a time when labor came into acute awareness of their increasing powerlessness within the developing International Division of Cultural Labor (Miller, Govil, McMurria, & Maxwell, 2001), with much time spent trying to exert some political or economic control over this process—with little overall success.

Themes of class tension and industry de-territorialization would continue in discussions of runaway film production in the 1960s, but with intensified debates over runaway industry extravagance, the long-term impact of free trade agreements, and the appropriate role of Congress in regulating the U.S. motion picture industry through domestic and foreign policy.

NOTES

1. Portions of this chapter were first published in the following article, and appear in this book courtesy of Taylor & Francis (www.tandfonline.com): Johnson-Yale, C. (2015). Frozen in Hollywood: Postwar Film Policy and the New Power-Geometry of Globalizing Production Labor. *Critical Studies in Media Communication, 32*(1), 33–47. doi:10.1080/15295036.2014.998251.

2. NATTKE was the British equivalent of the IATSE, representing below-the-line film, television, and stage labor in the United Kingdom. NATTKE joined the Association of Broadcasting Staff in 1984 to become the Broadcasting and Entertainment Trades Alliance (BETA). In 1991, BETA was merged into the Broadcasting, Entertainment, Cinematograph and Theatre Union (BECTU), which is still in place as of this writing.

3. *Salt of the Earth* (1954) is perhaps the most famous example of a McCarthy-era film that was banned by the industry at large because of its supposedly pro-communist content. Based on a true story, the film depicts a protracted labor strike against a zinc mine in New Mexico. The film's writer, Michael Wilson, was blacklisted, but continued to produce several successful scripts either anonymously or pseudonymously, including *Bridge on the River Kwai* (1957) and *Lawrence of Arabia* (1962). Herbert J. Biberman, the director of *Salt of the Earth*, was among the "Hollywood Ten" who had refused to testify before the House Un-American Activities Committee in 1947, and was sent to jail for contempt of Congress.

4. The U.S. weekly theater attendance peaked at 80 million in 1946—its highest point in motion picture history (Segrave, 1999, p. 5).

5. Extras usually fall to the bottom of the Screen Actors pay scale. Even in the 2000s, extras typically earn a flat rate of $100 or less a day, with shoot days averaging around fourteen hours.

Chapter Two

Cleopatra Conquers Rome

Runaway Blockbusters in the 1960s

The 1960s were a time of significant political and cultural upheaval. And as a culture industry, Hollywood was not immune to the social disturbances rippling across the United States during this era. Though the Cold War raged on in Washington, Hollywood's anti-communist fervor weakened significantly in the first part of the decade: in 1960, screenwriter Dalton Trumbo openly defied the blacklist, working under his own name for the first time since his conviction for contempt of court in the 1947 Hollywood HUAC hearings (Weiler, 1960); and in 1964, Stanley Kubrick's Cold War satire *Dr. Strangelove, Or: How I Learned to Stop Worrying and Love the Bomb* (1964) found its way onto the best picture nominee list of the Academy Awards. But despite lagging credibility for McCarthyism politics in Hollywood—a cornerstone of postwar runaway production debates—Hollywood labor regrouped and intensified their campaign against runaway film production in the 1960s. Their approach included two primary understandings of the issue: as a problem created by runaway media trade regulation and anticompetitive economic incentives abroad, and as a result of runaway film budgets and lifestyles of Hollywood's top talent.

The first theme, Runaway Trade, is argued to represent competing, yet interdependent, constructs of global "de-territorialization" and "re-territorialization." According to Negus and Román-Velázquez (2000), de-territorialization represents globalization as a positive force for "creating 'new markets,' breaking down barriers, and disrupting previous routines" (p. 329). Throughout the 1960s, Hollywood's producers and owners employed a discourse of de-territorialization as a justification for their production ventures abroad. At the same time, it was also used as a critique of Hollywood labor unions and their seemingly blind dedication to outmoded production routines, such as recreating foreign locations on Hollywood's soundstages. Hollywood film labor, on the other hand, is argued to have adopted a discourse of re-territorialization, calling for the reinstatement and reconstitution of Hollywood's localized identity—as a production community, as a political touchstone, and as a cinematic locale—in relation to the global (Canclini, 1995, p. 229).

The second theme, Runaway Extravagance, is examined through Doreen Massey's (1994) theory of labor mobility and spatial distribution. Massey contends that we must look not only at who is or is not mobile within the global flows and interconnections of capital, but also who has power in relation to these flows. The Runaway Extravagance debates of the 1960s are argued to represent labor's growing frustration over the increasing power of Hollywood's elite, including actors, to initiate the flows and movements of film productions overseas, while labor's power to influence the flow of production back to Hollywood was being continually diminished.

A lively and contentious counter discourse to runaway film production also appeared in the 1960s. Several Hollywood directors, producers, and actors championed creative runaways—productions staged overseas or outside Hollywood based on a need for location authenticity. Production labor had long considered location authenticity a reasonable motivation for filming outside Hollywood. However, labor began to question such explanations as mere subterfuge for avoidance of Hollywood union pay scales, growing dependence on European film industry subsidies, and lifestyle accommodations for Hollywood's rich and famous living and working abroad. As with the theme of Runaway Extravagance, the conceptual tug-o-war over the meaning and function of Creative Runaways in the 1960s served as an expression of a power struggle within the power geometry of global film production. Only in this instance, the struggle over foreign production for location authenticity was as much about controlling the "mediascape"—the global sphere in which images of the world are produced—as it was about controlling the "financescape," or the global flows of capital and labor (Appadurai, 1996).

THE TRADE REGULATION DEBATE

With the negotiation of the Bretton Woods Agreement in 1944, and the subsequent creation of the General Agreement on Tariffs and Trade (GATT) in 1947, the development and regulation of free trade became one of the most—if not *the* most—important global initiatives for the United States following the war. And not surprisingly, free trade had been a significant underlying issue within the runaway production debates over the Anglo-American Film Pacts of 1948 and 1950. By the 1960s, Hollywood industry owners and producers argued that trade liberalization had become more than a quest for new markets and industry expansion as it was constructed in the postwar years, but rather as a matter of survival for their industry. According to their assessment, since World War II, Hollywood had become increasingly dependent on foreign revenues to keep its domestic industry afloat; and through this logic, so-called runaway production was just part of the trade deal required to gain access to vital European markets. Hollywood labor, however, did not buy into the urgency of free trade to their domestic industry, nor did they see it as their duty to be the sacrificial lamb for Hollywood's global trade initiatives. On the contrary, Hollywood labor saw the push for trade liberalization as an excuse for producers to "run" from U.S. unionized labor, ultimately serving as a cause, and not a cure, for domestic unemployment in the U.S. film industry.

The debates over runaway free trade and runaway production would play out over several important events in the 1960s, including a special Congressional Hearing on Imports and Exports in 1961. It is at this point that we begin to see the Hollywood film industry grapple with the notion of media as cultural commodities, and the subsequent treatment of such commodities and their industries within global trade policy. For many countries in Europe, the understanding of media as cultural commodities was (and continues to be) the standing rationale for the implementation of subsidies and quotas to protect their national media industries from American cultural imperialism (Christopherson, 2005; Hoskins, Finn, & McFayden, 1996; Miller, Govil, McMurria, & Maxwell, 2001). Hollywood trade interests such as the MPAA staunchly opposed such cultural definitions of media, and the protectionist measures that accompanied them, as incompatible with global capitalism and trade liberalization; motion pictures and television programs were no different than any other commodities being traded on the global free market, and should stand on their own without government intervention. Hollywood labor, however, countered that comparable subsidies were needed in the United States to maintain the cultural integrity of American films and TV content in danger of being compromised by foreign runaway productions.

The 1961 Congressional Hearings on Imports and Exports

In September 1959, the Hollywood AFL Film Council launched their newest lobbying campaign with the publication of a brochure titled "The World's Sneakiest Smuggler." The brochure, distributed to all members of the AFL-CIO preceding their convention in San Francisco that year, presented a dire picture of the runaway film production problem for American labor, claiming that as much as 50 percent of all Hollywood features and made-for-TV movies were being filmed outside the United States (AFL Film Council Intensifies, 1959). The Council recommended the boycott of such foreign-made films by the AFL-CIO membership, and presented a resolution at the convention calling for the drafting of federal legislation that would require runaway films to be prominently labelled with their film location in the titles and in related marketing materials.

By fall of 1961, labor had made a few allies on Capitol Hill, most notably House Representative John Dent (D-PA). As chairman of the Education and Labor subcommittee on Imports and Exports, Dent was intrigued with the issue of runaway film production as further evidence of an overall need for a Reciprocal Trade Act—legislation that would counter the free trade agenda of big business and tighten the requirements for access to the U.S. market by foreign competitors (Lewis, 1961). Government subsidies for foreign film industries, stiff import quotas on American films, and frozen funds policies for U.S. exhibition revenues had long been thorns in the side of anti-runaway lobbyists in Hollywood—all were seen to exacerbate foreign runaway film production in one way or another. By contrast, there were no comparable restrictions on foreign production companies who wanted to do business with—or in—the United States.

Leading up to the hearings, *Variety* editor Thomas Pryor[1] wrote a three-part series on the issue of runaway film production, anticipating arguments that would be made by Hollywood management, talent, and labor (Pryor, 1961, November 15). He began by arguing the centrality of the Screen Actors Guild to issues of runaway production: first, that some viewed the personal finances and lifestyle choices of Hollywood stars as responsible for the trend toward overseas location shooting; and second, that some viewed the high cost of hiring extras in Hollywood as driving large-scale productions to shoot where they could have access to inexpensive "atmosphere." Other debated causes of runaway production included cost-prohibitive union contracts in Hollywood and the subsequent lure of cost-saving subsidy plans overseas.

Pryor's sympathies were clearly on the side of labor. In his last installment in the runaway production series, he expressed his concerns for the future of Hollywood's industry, and frustration with those who seemed to dismiss the seriousness of the threat of overseas production (Pryor, 1961, November 17, p. 1). He predicted that producers and above-the-line talent would remain relatively unscathed by the overseas trend, whereas the outcome appeared bleaker for Hollywood's below-the-line labor, who faced the loss of eligibility for industry pension plans and psychological trauma due to long term unemployment. In Pryor's final assessment, anyone who thought that Hollywood could remain on top of the industry while sending more and more productions overseas were "talking through their hats" (p. 1).

The Congressional hearings by the House Education and Labor subcommittee were held in the capital throughout November and December of 1961.

They were meant to provide a forum for leaders from several industries, including agriculture, transportation, chemical, oil, and motion picture production, to air their concerns about the impact of foreign trade practices on employment conditions in the U.S. Hollywood industry leaders turned out in full force for the hearings, including representatives from the major unions, actors, and industry executives, including the venerable Eric Johnston of the MPAA.

The inclusion of the motion picture industry in the Congressional hearings was the first point of contention between Hollywood's free trade and anti-runaway production factions. The AFL Film Council had lobbied hard for inclusion of the film industry in the hearings in order to frame runaway production and labor outsourcing as common denominators with more traditional American industries, like manufacturing (Sherman, 1961). Representatives of Hollywood's executive class, however, played up the seeming incongruity of the film industry's presence among the other industries, arguing that the problems of glittery Hollywood could hardly be as severe or imminent as those affecting the U.S. rust and grain belts. Eric Johnston was the first industry representative to testify, and immediately set to the task of delegitimizing the seriousness of Hollywood's foreign production problems as compared to other industrial communities: "Now, I've heard Hollywood called many things, but I don't think it can yet be called a depressed area" (Hearings before the Subcommittee, 1962, p. 464). Gone were Johnston's sympathies for the plight of film labor so often experessed in his IATSE convention speeches. This was purely about business, and Johnston was in his element as a seasoned trade and policy negotiator. After taking a jab at the "depressed" lifestyles of Hollywood, Johnston went on to describe how the U.S. film industry had in fact become utterly dependent, rather than deeply undermined, by foreign production and theater revenues. With the rise of independent producers, he explained that much of the control over selection of motion picture production locations had been lost by the Hollywood majors, and subsequently reduced the frequency of productions in their Hollywood studios. Television was aslo cited as a major contributing factor in the decline of Hollywood's film industry, with many people staying home rather than going out to the movies as was the pre-World War II practice. With a weakened domestic market, Johnston argued that foreign distribution and production had become Hollywood's bread and butter. But access and dependence on these new European markets had their price: ". . . if we expect to sell in the foreign market, we must engage in business in the foreign market" (p. 465).

And thus, Johnston defended the choice of some Hollywood producers to make films abroad, countering that the phrase "runaway production" misrepresented both the loyalties of his colleagues to the American industry and the nature of international film production and trade. Johnston also opposed trade restrictions, defending the ongoing efforts to establish reciprocal film trade policies between U.S. and European film industries. Congressman John Ashbrook (R-OH) challenged Johnston on this point, noting that the term "reciprocal" was something of a misnomer in light of European trade restrictions, such as film quotas, and suggesting with a bit of cynicism that perhaps "unreciprocal reciprocal agreements" would be a more accurate description (p. 472). Johnston assured Ashbrook and the other committee members that, with continued pressure from the U.S. government, European markets would eventually become completely open. He provided evidence of several markets, including the UK, that had loosened their trade policies since the war.

Johnston's testimony was followed by two additional representatives of Hollywood's free trade contingent: Griffith Johnson, vice president of the MPAA and Motion Picture Export Association of America, and Charles S. Boren, executive vice president of the Association of Motion Picture Producers. Each provided extensive quantitative evidence to support Johnston's testimony, with Johnson discussing and comparing figures on American and foreign film imports and exports, and Boren addressing employment and production trends in Hollywood (Hearings before the Subcommittee, 1962). By their estimations, Hollywood was still very much on top of the global game in terms of production and distribution prowess. And despite the decline in motion picture production in the wake of television's expansion, their data also showed conditions for Hollywood labor remaining relatively stable, in part due to the increased demand for telefilms (aka made-for-TV movies). Griffith Johnson's only warning to the committee was that Hollywood labor would likely experience a second stagnation in coming years due to the increased implementation of trade barriers against U.S. telefilms. With such barriers being erected, American production companies would again be forced to enter reciprocal agreements, likely including telefilm production abroad, in order to retain access to fast-growing foreign television markets (pp. 481–82).

Members of the AFL Film Council testified next, firing back at the industry executives and their construction of the foreign film trade situation. H. O'Neil Shanks, executive secretary of the Screen Extras Guild and chairman of the Foreign Film Committee of the Hollywood AFL Film Council, addressed the committee first, flanked by fellow Councilmen John W. Lehners of the Motion Picture Film Editors union and IATSE attorney Robert W. Gilbert. Shanks presented three major arguments for Congressional intervention in the film industry's runaway problems: first, that contrary to Eric Johnston's statement, runaway production was indeed a national concern, with the export of film jobs not only affecting Hollywood and California labor, but labor in New York and other states as well; second, that the bolstering of foreign production was potentially jeopardizing Hollywood's standing as the world leader in film production; and finally, that runaway production was undermining the United States's ability to utilize film as a global emissary for democracy, and perhaps even aiding in the spread of communism—a continuation of the "un-American" theme employed in runaway production debates in the 1950s. Shanks elaborated on this final point, suggesting that some runaway producers were actually "surrendering control of content with respect to pictures made abroad and cooperating with Communist-controlled unions" (pp. 498–89). And while salvaging jobs for American film laborers was their practical concern, the Council members argued that the fight against runaway production was also a fight against communism.

The Labor and Education subcommittee was presented with a hefty report compiled by the AFL Film Council, addressing the present and future impact of runaway film production on Hollywood (p. 497). Relying heavily on data provided in Irving Bernstein's *Hollywood at a Crossroads* (1957), the Council report painted a very different picture of exhibition and production trends in Hollywood, pointing out, for instance, that twelve of sixteen films shown in Los Angeles theaters in September 1961 had been "American-aspect" foreign productions, along with all four Best Picture Oscar winners from 1956 to 1959. The report meticulously addressed the four primary reasons provided by producers for filming abroad: location authenticity, frozen funds access, establishing goodwill with foreign markets, and competitive production costs. While the Film Council agreed that some films required location shooting, they took a much harder line on creative runaways than in the past. Their report contended that the vast majority of those American-backed foreign productions claiming location authenticity were actually running away from union and guild contracts (Hearings before the Subcommittee, 1962, p. 505), with some filmmakers accused of spending weeks or months shooting on sound stages in Europe after location work was completed (p. 507). Jack Dales of the Screen Actors Guild followed up by asking, "whatever happened to the second unit to shoot foreign exteriors, with interiors made in Hollywood?" The 1961 release *Judgment at Nuremberg*, shot in Hollywood with German location footage spliced in, was provided as a successful example of this strategy.

Labor leaders quickly dismissed the producers' contentions that frozen funds and "goodwill" productions accounted for the majority of overseas productions, and were justifiable. But the AFL Film Council pounced on this assertion, citing Eric Johnston's own testimony in which he stated that revenue blockages in Europe had been greatly reduced since the postwar years. And more specifically, in the eleven years since the Anglo-American Film Pact of 1951, frozen "coin" policies had been completely removed by the four nations most engaged in film production and trade with U.S. producers: the United Kingdom, France, Italy, and Germany (p. 507). The AFL Film Council treated the "goodwill" and "good business" explanations for runaway production as similarly unfounded. They argued that if foreign production was necessary to the economic survival and global appeal of Hollywood—supposedly the most vital and popular production center in the world—then why weren't filmmakers from weaker and lesser known European film markets travelling to the United States for the same reason? Alternately, Italian studios were said to be so booked with American productions that U.S. producers were "beginning to step on each others' toes" (p. 508). And yet Italian filmmakers were nowhere to be seen in the United States. Finally, labor argued that if the point of American production abroad was to spread good will to all countries around the world, then why were so many productions concentrated in the same four European countries with relatively well-established film industries? The Council concluded that "shooting on foreign locations to build good will . . . is a dubious point when you figure out the cost, the troubles, and the economic injury and bad will created here" (p. 509).

The final reason for foreign production challenged in the report was "comparative production costs." This was a much more sensitive subject for Hollywood's labor than the others because more often than not, exhorbitant union contracts at home were blamed for American producers running abroad. The Council once again deferred to Irving Bernstein's findings in the *Crossroads* report to counter such claims. Bernstein suggested that only spectacle or blockbuster films requiring extraordinary numbers of extras really experienced a labor cost benefit by producing abroad; for all others, the benefit was marginal (p. 510). Labor next discussed the subsidy structure in place in European film production markets, which often provided U.S. filmmakers with the same cost-saving benefits as indigenous productions. The report explained that European subsidies were driven by a heightened sense of the importance of film industries to their national economic and cultural welfare compared to the United States. Subsequently, they argued that European countries had felt the need to create additional protections for their industries through the implementation of subsidies, screen quotas, and currency restrictions. By contrast, motion picture production in the United States was treated as a private enterprise and afforded no special government protections (p. 511). Labor contended that the European film industry subsidies were being justified as a protective measure against competition from Hollywood—both as a formidable economic force and a cultural influence. From labor's perspective, however, the cultural and economic protectionist argument was a pretense to justify anti-competitive subsidies that would create more runaway production from Hollywood; and if the foreign subisidies were meant to protect local culture and film production from Hollywood, why were U.S. film interests allowed to co-produce projects with them?

The AFL Film Council report concluded with a list of recommended solutions for ending Hollywood's runaway problems, to be implemented by Congress. The Council first called for a special Congressional investigation of runaway production, arguing that a government probe would benefit from the "power of the subpoena" for accessing overseas production records, which the Council lacked. They urged the committee to investigate personal earnings and tax filings of runaway producers and actors, as well as any overseas corporations they owned that might function as tax shelters; Otto Preminger, director-producer of the Israel-based *Exodus* (1960), and Samuel Bronston, producer of the Italy- and Spain-based *El Cid* (1961), were of interest in this regard (p. 514). Several legislative measures were also suggested, including government loans and subsidies for the U.S. film industry, the labeling and placement of import restrictions on foreign-produced films, and legal ramifications for employers running abroad to avoid union contracts (pp. 415–17).

Members of the Screen Actors Guild were among the last to testify on the matter of runaway film production before the Congressional committee. Interestingly, their position on the issue departed somewhat from that of other production labor. This was mostly because actors had been consistently accused by the unions of running abroad to receive tax breaks, as in the case of the 18-month tax rule, or to accommodate political or lifestyle choices. John L. Dales, executive national secretary of the Guild and member of the AFL Film Council, defended the members of his union before the labor committee. He argued that actors were being used as a scapegoat for runaway production, and that he could find only six or seven cases where an actor might be overseas for tax purposes (p. 617). Dales assured the committee members that the most detrimental factor in creating runaway production was foreign industry subsidies and tax advantages to producers, and not actors.

As vice president of the Screen Actors Guild, Charlton Heston also stepped forward to defend actors' participation in foreign productions, mostly arguing that the internationalization of the U.S. film industry made such choices inevitable. In his testimony before the Congressional Subcommittee, Heston introduced himself as "a migrant worker," continuing with a tongue-in-cheek assessment of the transient life of the actor (Hearings before the Subcommittee, 1962, p. 620). In response to the argument that actors wanted to work overseas to maintain extravagant lifestyles, Heston described his own grueling experiences making films abroad: Climbing Mt. Sinai in bare feet, working sixty-hour workweeks in Rome shooting physically demanding chariot scenes (p. 621). It was far from glamorous and extravagant, and by his estimation, most actors would prefer to go home to their own bed at night rather than a hotel. But while Heston supported measures that would stimulate domestic production, he felt that restrictions on foreign production were not the answer. Rather, he aligned his position with producers and investors who had long insisted that the health of Hollywood's industry was closely tied to foreign production, and restrictions would only hurt an already weakened domestic industry.

The outcome of the hearings for the motion picture industry was mixed. The Congressional subcommittee recommended an official investigation, but made no immediate legislative actions on behalf of labor; the banner headline in *Variety* following the hearings declared that "Economics, and not Patriotism" (1961, p. 3) had ruled the day. And yet, the meaning of the headline extended well beyond the context of the Congressional hearings. Throughout the 1950s, Hollywood executives had argued that it was postwar patriotism and a commitment to the recovery of our wartime allies that had driven the trend in overseas film production. By the 1960s, the argument of European dependence had been replaced by a discourse of global economic interdependence; that Hollywood producers were being driven by the quest for new markets to support the domestic film industry, without which the domestic industry would surely fail—a central component within the theory of global de-territorialization (Negus & Román-Velázquez, 2000).

Hollywood labor had made their own efforts to de-territorialize their industry in order to gain the support of the Congressional committee. By acknowledging other production communities in the United States, they had attempted to construct runaway production as an American problem and not just a Hollywood problem. This was a tough sell, as the identity of the motion picture industry was (and continues to be) so intrinsically linked to the locality of Hollywood. And while the 1961 Congressional hearings played an important role in raising awareness among federal officials of the issue of runaway film production, few in Congress were willing to take up the cause of Hollywood unemployment over industries closer to voters' day-to-day lives, such as auto production and agriculture. But in the years to come, runaway production would in fact become a more salient issue for state and local politicians, particularly as a campaign platform in California.

Labor's Congressional lobbying for film industry subsidies touched off some heated commentary in the press, particularly from directors and producers explicitly or implicitly labeled as "runaways" during testimonies. Otto Preminger, a vocal critic of the anti-communist and anti-runaway lobbies in Hollywood,[2] saw government subsidies as incompatible with the American business tradition of competition in a free market. His blunt assessment was, "If we are not good enough to compete in the world market we are not good enough" (Williams, 1961, p. 19). Preminger instead blamed domestic industry problems on out-of-control union contracts and lack of leadership. He derided the unions for their shortsighted understanding of Hollywood and its film industry, declaring both to be undeniably international (p. 19). Fed up with the "racket" of production in Hollywood and the United States, Preminger had declared his intention to work "away from Hollywood" from that point forward. Members of the Writers' Guild of America also came out against the AFL Film Council's campaign for subsidies and quotas, with West coast president Charles Schnee accusing the Council of running a "headline-hunting attack" against the U.S. film industry (Shanks, Lehners, & Gilbert, 1961). The Council defended their position and restated their case in a letter to the *Los Angeles Times*, explaining that in light of failed attempts to engage management on the matter of runaway film production and deal with the problem internally, outside assistance from the government—possibly in the form of subsidies—was considered a necessity.

Organized Hollywood labor and management groups attempted to put aside their differences after the Congressional hearings and collaborate on a domestic industry agenda to abate runaway production practices. In the spring 1962, the Hollywood Joint Labor-Management Committee on Foreign Film Production was formed, comprised of members of the AFL Film Council and the Association of Motion Picture Producers. The committee created a list of possible industry policies and legislative actions that might slow the foreign production trend, primarily focusing on individual and industry level tax reforms (Plans Offered to Lessen, 1962). After petitioning the Department of Labor for a federal investigation of runaway film production, Labor Secretary W. Willard Wirtz appointed Assistant Secretary George Weaver to work with the Joint Committee to determine if federal assistance was needed (Wirtz appoints board, 1963). The Hollywood labor-management group presented their list of concerns and possible solutions to Weaver and several leading legislators in California, including Senator Kuchel (Film Unions Seek, 1963). In particular, they recommended a federal subsidy for domestic production to counteract the effects of foreign industry subsidies, to be implemented through the recycling of federal movie admissions taxes back into the U.S. film industry. Assistant Secretary Weaver organized a preliminary investigation of runaway production in response, so that a more informed decision on potential legislation could be made. However, the investigation dissolved in early 1964 with the demise of the Hollywood Joint Labor-Management committee: by February that year, a majority of producers active in the joint committee had shifted their support in favor of foreign production practices, necessitating a split from labor and the AFL Film Council in their pursuit of industry subsidies ("Runaway" Film Joint Committee, 1964). With Congressional interest in the issue waning, momentum was clearly amassing behind global trade and production initiatives, and not economic protectionism.

While organized film labor struggled to gain federal support against runaway production, their efforts at the state level found more traction. In California, labor interests appealed to the state senate for tax relief for productions staged in Hollywood in order to keep up with tax incentives offered abroad. Until 1963, films had been taxed by local assessors on both their tangible and intangible value: tangible value included basic costs for production, such as film stock and equipment rentals; intangible value included the estimated worth of scripts, film rights, and "star value" (Ostrow, 1963, p. B7). The proposed Rees Tax Relief Bill would do away with taxes on intangible value—perhaps the largest portion of the tax burden for producers—which labor groups hoped would attract production back to Hollywood. With an amendment added that would give local assessors the authority to determine what would be considered tangible or intangible—and ultimately taxable—the bill passed through the California State Assembly. But despite majority approval, some state legislators and local assessors vehemently opposed the bill, arguing that the anticipated burden on the local economy by the film tax exemption would far outweigh the benefits to the industry. Calling the runaway film production argument a "smoke screen," County Tax Assessor Philip E. Watson probed at what he saw as the extraordinary injustice of the bill: why should homeowners with properties worth $20,000 or less be assessed at a substantially higher tax rate than a $40 million blockbuster like *Cleopatra*? (Brown Asked to Veto, 1963, p. 24). Closed-door sessions were held with Governor Edmund "Pat" Brown later in June. The sessions were attended by Assessor Watson and several assemblypersons arguing against the Film Tax Exemption Bill, as well as several industry leaders in favor of the bill including Charles Boren of the Association of Motion Picture Producers and IATSE president Pat Somerset (Brown Ponders Bill, 1963). Governor Brown ultimately vetoed the bill based on the estimated loss of tax revenues, but called for a special commission to study the film industry problem for a possible redrafting of the bill in 1964 (Lembke, 1963).

As it would happen, Governor Brown's reluctance to support the Rees Tax Bill and runaway film production relief played out to his advantage in 1964. That spring, a series of reports were published suggesting the domestic industry had turned a corner, with the number of productions staged in Hollywood estimated to be 25 percent higher than the previous year (Smith, 1964, June 16; Smith, 1964, June 15). Several explanations were provided for the resurgence, including increased domestic telefilm production, rising theater attendance, and increased overseas production costs. By 1965, production in Hollywood was reported to be so strong, some producers even expressed concern over the availability of studio space (Bart, 1965, July 10), fueling yet another runaway production panic over the increased efforts by other states to attract overflow production work from Hollywood, includng New York (Garrigues, 1966). Hollywood was officially fighting a "two front" war against runaway film production, with competition for production dollars coming from locations both foreign and domestic. And while non-union contracts were the primary concern for Hollywood labor regarding domestic competition in the 1960s, subsidies would eventually enter into debates over domestic runaway film production in the decades to come.

By the end of the 1960s, Hollywood labor had made very little headway with their ongoing battle with runaway production and trade. Proposals for federal and state subsidies for the film industry had consistently met with diffidence—even in California where the industry represented an important sector of the state's economy. A major hurdle for labor was the need to re-territorialize Hollywood production as a local, if not national, cultural industry in need of protective economic policies. According to Hollywood's ownership and management class, the genie was already out of the bottle. Hollywood production was already effectively a globalized and de-territorialized industry (Negus & Román-Velázquez, 2000); more a commodifiable production process than a place or space of production. Massey (1994) has described how re-territorialization efforts by labor are often rejected within classical liberal models of economy as provincial, reactionary, and even a form of romanticized escapism from the realities of globalizing industry (p. 151). In the debates over runaway trade, Hollywood labor were similarly constructed as naïve to the realities of global industry and production, as well as to the nature of "real" economic strife experienced by labor in other "real" industries such as agriculture and manufacturing.

A second major hurdle for labor within the runaway trade debates had been the persistent myth of industry extravagance. Hollywood owners and their representatives had consistently referenced their industry's glossy reputation as evidence of its financial soundness, despite the extraordinary disparity between above- and below-the-line wages.[3] Regardless of its accuracy, it was an effective strategy for dampening interest among state and federal legislators in supporting film industry subsidies: even if labor was correct and the Hollywood production sector was in serious trouble because of free trade policies and runaway production, who would be the one to champion industry subsidies for Hollywood—the land of swimming pools and movie stars? Interestingly enough, Hollywood's below-the-line labor would turn the argument of industry extravagance back on above-the-line labor by focusing on the extravagant lifestyles of Hollywood's elite living overseas as a major cause of runaway film production in the 1960s.

"GO BIG OR GO HOME!"

Blockbusters had become increasingly important to the Hollywood film industry in the 1950s and 1960s as a way to compete with television. Films such as *Lawrence of Arabia* (1962), *Dr. Zhivago* (1965), and *The Sound of Music* (1965) took full advantage of the "big screen" by using Cinemascope and other widescreen formats to dazzle audiences with epic tales set in exotic landscapes; something that television was unable to offer on its small, black-and-white screen.[4] Blockbusters also provided long term employment for some Hollywood film labor, mostly above-the-line actors, directors, producers, and other key technical crew, who were often working on such films for over a year. But blockbusters presented new and unexpected problems for many below-the-line workers whose jobs could easily be filled on-site. As was discussed in the previous chapter, many producers argued that it was cost prohibitive to shoot blockbusters in Hollywood due to the high cost of using union extras; and blockbusters typically required thousands of extras to populate their signature, epic battle scenes and crowd scenes. On the other end of the spectrum, blockbuster films were heavily dependent on big-name movie stars and directors for their marketing strategies. And it was Hollywood labor's concern that these individuals were exercising an incredible amount of influence over how—and more importantly to the runaway production debates, where—films would be made. Specifically, it was argued that actors and directors were driving productions abroad to accommodate their indulgent, globe-trotting lifestyles.

The runaway extravagance debates in the 1960s are argued to reflect what Massey (1994) has described as the "power geometry" of globalizing industry. In relation to the global flows of capital and resources, Massey explains that "[d]ifferent social groups have distinct relationships to this anyway differentiated mobility: some people are more in charge of it than others; some initiate flows and movements, others don't; some are effectively imprisoned by it" (p. 149). Those in charge are described more specifically as "the jet-setters, the ones sending and receiving the faxes and the e-mail, holding the international conference calls, the ones distributing the films, controlling the news, organizing the investments and the international currency transactions" (p. 149). When applied to the film industry in the 1960s, the runaway extravagance debates appear to have served as an expression of the frustration felt by Hollywood's below-the-line labor as they became "imprisoned" by the decisions of Hollywood's jet-set—decisions that often seemed capricious and self-indulgent, and lacking in concern for their potentially negative effect on the "home" industry.

Runaway Cleopatra

Hollywood labor singled out one film as the archetype of the runaway extravagance problem—the Egyptian melodrama *Cleopatra* (1963). Shot entirely on location in London and Rome, the film had taken almost three years to make, had gone over budget by $42 million,[5] and left 20th Century Fox on the verge of bankruptcy (Tribune Series Will Tell, 1963). Much of the blame for the film's problems was placed on its star, Elizabeth Taylor, whose erratic and self-indulgent behavior on set would become legendary within the industry. Production notes from the film describe almost daily shooting delays due to sudden illnesses and various other "unavailabilities" (Wanger & Hyams, 1963). An article in the *Los Angeles Times* described how incessant filming delays had unexpectedly pushed the production schedule into the winter months, causing concern that *Cleopatra*'s papier mâché sets would be destroyed by winter storms (Gris, 1960). Industry reporter Henri Gris concluded, "Hollywood has learned a bitter lesson. . . . Nothing of this would have happened had the picture gone before the cameras in sunny, if smoggy, Hollywood" (p. F3). *Cleopatra* was a modest commercial success and won four production-related Oscars in 1963. Film critics generally panned the film for historical inaccuracies and subpar performances. Hollywood's below-the-line labor referenced the film as a cautionary tale of the misguided logic and potentially disastrous consequences of runaway blockbusters and their out-of-control stars.

Elizabeth Taylor's overseas antics continued to serve as fodder for Hollywood's anti-runaway contingent well into the 1960s. One article reported that Taylor had insisted that three consecutives films be staged in Europe so that she could remain close to her husband, Richard Burton, while he also worked overseas (Browning, 1968). Browning described the extraordinary lengths to which one film—*The Only Game in Town*—had gone to accommodate Taylor, recreating Las Vegas (where the film was set) in Paris (where Taylor was residing): "Since there's nothing in Paris that even remotely resembles Las Vegas, they had to fly over cases of doorknobs, bathroom fixtures, carpets, slot machines, and even parking meters from the United States to Paris" (p. B7). The story was accompanied by a picture of Taylor with the simple caption: "The Runaway."

Some actors sided with Hollywood film crews and their contention that the personal indulgences of the industry's elite, and not location authenticity, were driving the trend in foreign production. Acting legend Bette Davis, who made her name in the 1930s during the Golden Age of Hollywood studio production, scoffed at the idea that location authenticity was so strongly influencing the industry:

> You do not go to motion pictures to see scenery. You go to see acting. You cannot do your best acting on location. They just go overseas today because

they have fun. You know, I have a feeling they have an absolute ball in Europe. (Hopper, 1962, October 18, p. C3)

Alfred Hitchcock held similar views on the real motivations for runaway production. As he commented during an acceptance speech at the 1965 Screen Producers Guild banquet, "There's only one way to stop runaway production, that is by persuading producers and directors to be faithful to their wives" (Producers Pick, 1965, p. A4). Screenwriter Ernest Lehman, who had penned Hitchcock's *North by Northwest* (1959), took a similarly derisive view when he created a list of nineteen "suggestions" for how to stop runaway productions, including renaming Santa Monica beach the Riviera, making boarding school mandatory for all "Hollywood children" over a year old, and providing an "interlocutory decree" for all married, male actors, writers, directors, and producers over age 40 (Lehman, 1962, p. 49).

While Hitchcock and Lehman could find humor in the situation, some actors took exception with the idea that working overseas was a mere indulgence. Instead, they argued that they were simply doing their job and were in no position to insist on shooting in the States given the tenuous nature of their work. In a commentary piece written for the *Hollywood Reporter* titled "'Runaway' of Necessity," Western star Van Heflin (1962) meticulously address the most pointed criticisms of runaway actors working abroad, including the old "tax cure" argument. By his estimation, an actor's career, like the career of a professional athlete, had a limited shelf life; they could be a box office hit one day and a flop the next. For this reason, Heflin supported the choice of some actors to seek tax protections for their earnings, including foreign residency. These were common practices among managers and owners in more traditional industries, such as textiles and oil production. And yet, he argued, actors were treated as though they were being self-indulgent rather than demonstrating business savvy as in those other industries. Interestingly, Heflin conceded to labor's perspective that Hollywood had become too reliant on risky, multi-million-dollar extravaganzas. Specifically, he questioned the practice of relying too heavily on "name" actors to buoy otherwise mediocre projects—a criticism that appeared directed at *Cleopatra*, in production at the time. Instead he called for producers to return to making "quality productions on a sensible budget," regardless of their location.

In fact, the Screen Actors Guild made some earnest efforts in the early 1960s to address their possible contribution to runaway industry extravagance and runaway production. Near the end of 1962, the Guild's membership, mostly comprised of thousands of modestly paid, unknown players, voted for a moratorium on pay raises to attract producers back to Hollywood. Producer-director Stanley Kramer, whose work included *The Caine Mutiny* (1954) and *Judgment at Nuremberg* (1961), applauded the Guild's efforts. Yet he acknowledged that the problem was not so much with the "little people," but with producers who regularly overbid stars' salaries, and the stars themselves who demanded above-scale compensation for their work. Kramer challenged stars to scale down their salary demands, while also encouraging producers to "have the guts" to cast unknown talent (Self-searching in the Movies, 1962, p. A4).

But contrary to Kramer's assessment, the Screen Actors Guild also saw problems with the way salaries of the "little people," namely secondary players and background talent, were used as a bargaining chip by producers and directors of runaway blockbusters. George Steven's production of *The Greatest Story Ever Told* (1965) was a pivotal case, as the director had never "run" from the United States to make a picture. Even when making *The Diary of Anne Frank* (1959), Stevens had chosen to blend background images of Holland with Hollywood studio footage to keep the production stateside. But despite previous efforts, the director made it known that exorbitant Hollywood production costs—particularly for the thousands of required extras—were forcing him to move *Greatest Story* to Spain where background talent of "Biblical proportions" could be hired for a fraction of Hollywood union scale (Pryor, 1961, November 16). He also contended that Hollywood's wardrobe unions had blocked the importation of thousands of costumes for the film, insisting the garments be handmade for an estimated $145,000, compared to $7,500 in overseas wardrobe rentals (p. 1). Stevens' commentary on the *Greatest Story* predicament started a bargaining frenzy among Hollywood politicians trying to score points with local labor interests (Plot Hollywood's "Greatest Story," 1962). Los Angeles Mayor Sam Yorty became personally involved in lobbying efforts, promising Stevens a public celebration and show of gratitude if the film remained in Hollywood. George Stevens finally conceeded and signed deals with Hollywood's Screen Extras Guild and Costumers' union a few months later.

But George Stevens was an exception, as many directors and actors adamantly defended their choice to work abroad, even for reasons considered "indulgent" by Hollywood labor interests. After a long stint shooting in Paris for his film *How to Steal a Million Dollars* (1966), director William Wyler proclaimed to the press his disinterest in ever working in Hollywood again. He complained bitterly that Hollywood's nine-to-six union-mandated schedule had "appalling" effects on his actors' performances, as they were often required to report for hair and makeup as early as 6 a.m. to accommodate the schedule. And from his experience, the early hours were bad for both their appearance and the level of energy they brought to the set (Dart, 1966, p. 27). Wyler even ventured to argue that the more rigid Hollywood schedule encouraged bad behavior by actors, as they often chose to simply report late to work every day rather than adhere to the early hours—shutting down productions until they arrived. Wyler insisted that "running" to Europe and to a more leisurely noon to 7:30 p.m. schedule was a matter of necessity, not indulgence. And given the later start times on European shoots, he argued that he had greater expectations of actors while working overseas than in Hollywood; to support his claim, he described having fired George C. Scott from an overseas production for arriving to work five hours late.

While producers and actors may have agreed on the benefits of leisurely European production schedules, opinions diverged regarding the necessity of overseas production for talent recruitment. Producers maintained that foreign productions were important opportunities for recruiting and grooming fresh, European actors that would appeal to globalizing film audiences. In an interview with Hollywood columnist Hedda Hopper, film producer Walter Wanger contended that imported foreign talent like Marlene Deitrich and Maurice Chavalier were the reason Hollywood had dominated foreign markets for so long (Hopper, 1962, August 16). The goal was to have "world-wide appeal," and English and French producers who had stubbornly "stuck to their nationalism" according to Wanger, were now seeing the benefits of co-producing with the United States and using "outside" talent. He also explained that the roles of actors and producers in the production process were no longer as clearly delineated as they had been, and thus it was only natural to expect the stars to have more of a say in how and where productions occurred (p. C8).

Many Hollywood actors, however, were chafed by the competition from abroad. In 1963, the leadership of the Screen Actors Guild argued that runaway producers were creating bidding wars between U.S., U.K., and Canadian screen actors groups for telefilm projects, resulting in negotiated wages well under union scale for all three groups. SAG decided to address the problem by initiating negotiations of the Toronto Agreement: a collective bargaining agreement between the British Equity, the Irish Actors Equity, the American Screen Actors Guild, and the Association of Candian Television and Radio Artists. The agreement required telefilm producers to pay the same wage scales and abide by the same residual contracts in all participating countries—an attempt to discourage productions from "running" from one country to another in search of the best deal on secondary talent ("Runaway Film" Foreign Wage Pact, 1963). The unity amongst the three acting guilds, however, was short-lived.

By 1965, the Screen Actors Guild had begun consulting with federal labor and immigration agencies in search of possible options for barring overseas actors from working in Hollywood (Bart, 1965, February 7). Guild executive John Dales clarified that they were less concerned with the few "distinguished" actors like Alec Guinness who worked regularly in Hollywood, and more concerned with the trend of importing secondary talent from overseas (p. X7). Much like the runaway trade debates of the past, some Hollywood talent felt that foreign labor policies were non-reciprocal—foreign actors could work in Hollywood as they pleased, while Hollywood actors were sometimes barred from working for foreign production companies overseas. American icon Jack Palance argued that inequities also extended to the ways British and American actors were recognized for their achievements in either country: While actors from the U.K. can compete alongside American actors for a coveted Oscar, American actors can only be considered for best foreign actor in the U.K.'s industry awards (Harford, 1967, p. 16). These issues hit close to home for the actor—Palance was preparing for a film titled *Vegas 66,* with a five-week shooting schedule in Spain. He had no doubts that producers had chosen the location to take advantage of government subsidies and cheap Spanish talent. But he also placed the blame for such blatant runaway productions on the doorstep of the Screen Actors Guild, and challenged the SAG to find a way to remedy the situation (p. 16). But not all actors agreed with Palance. Some saw the internationalizing of Hollywood films as a natural and healthy process rather than a case of indulgence or European exceptionalism. British film star Laurence Harvey, who had portrayed an American in *The Manchurian Candidate* (1962), responded to industry criticisms of overseas productions and the possibility that he was himself a "lend-lease runaway" actor (Alpert, 1961). Calling the whole "runaway" issue nonsense, Harvey argued that he was neither running away from England or running to the United States, but rather "running with the times" and the new circumstances within the industry (p. Q10).

By the end of the decade, Hollywood's unions had become embattled in their fight against runaway actors and blockbusters. "Go big or go home!"—a saying often heard on film sets, even to this day—had become both a creative and economic touchstone for Hollywood's industry, with some of the most successful epics of all time being produced overseas in quick succession: *Doctor Zhivago* (1965) filmed in Spain; *The Dirty Dozen* (1967) filmed in England; and the beloved *Sound of Music* (1965) filmed on location in Germany and Austria. However, unions were still waiting to see the reciprocal creation of domestic jobs from these successful overseas extravaganzas, as runaway producers were often promising. Dwindling film and television projects in Hollywood suggested quite a different effect on their home industry. Robert Windeler (1968, January 8), a columnist for the *New York Times*, described Hollywood as "lively for a ghost town" (p. 127), with majors like MGM reporting their best earnings in over forty-five years, while their Hollywood studios were nearly vacant. The ongoing tensions between Hollywood's below-the-line labor and above-the-line actors over runaway production had caused a permanent rift between their respective unions and guilds. In 1965, the Screen Actors Guild officially left the Hollywood AFL Film Council, which had long been the primary organizing force against runaway production practices (King, 1965).

Another runaway trend of sorts also began to emerge in the late 1960s: high-profile actors began to "run" for political office—a rather explicit display of the authority actors were gaining within the "power geometry" of the New International Division of Cultural Labor (Massey, 1994; Miller, et al., 2001). The two most celebrated instances at the time were screen and stage star George Murphy, who became a California senator in 1964, and Ronald Reagan, who won his bid for governor of California in 1967. Murphy publicly stated his commitment to addressing the issue of runaway film production while in office (King L., 1967). Though Reagan did not specifically pledge support for anti-runaway production legislation upon entering office, many in the industry, including fellow member of the Motion Picture Industry Council and close friend, Roy Brewer, were heartened by his new position (McLellan, 2006). Perhaps not coincidentally, concerns over runaway actors subsided over the next decade. Instead, Hollywood's efforts against runaway production became increasingly dependent on the influence and support of actor-politicians on Capitol Hill—a trend that has endured into the twenty-first century.

"A Tree is a Tree, a Rock is a Rock. Shoot It in Griffith Park!"

Hollywood labor had always conceded the need to shoot some productions abroad for creative purposes, with the expectation that any scenes that did not depend on identifiable locations would be filmed in Hollywood. By the mid 1960s, however, Hollywood labor began to complain that many of these so-called "creative" runaway productions were engaging in economic runaway activities: filming interior scenes on less expensive foreign soundstages, employing locals as non-union extras, and even using foreign locations as stand-ins for U.S. locations when it was cost effective. Rather than deny the accusations, many of Hollywood's elite, including actors, producers, and directors, engaged in an organized and highly vocal defense of location authenticity shooting. They countered that Hollywood labor were out of their league when it came to understanding the more sophisticated tastes of modern audiences, as well as the more sophisticated political economy of a globalizing Hollywood film industry. Within this new world order, location choices were the domain of producers and directors, and Hollywood labor needed to learn their place and wait their turn.

The backlash from above-the-line labor over the issue of creative runaways also serves as another expression of their growing power within and in relation to the New International Division of Cultural Labor (Miller, et al., 2001). Specifically, it is argued to represent the growing dominance of corporate transculturalism as the guiding business ethos in Hollywood (Kraidy, 2005). Kraidy explains corporate transculturalism as an ideological vision of the world "in which fluid identities and porous cultural borders are depicted as growth engines in service of a cosmopolitan capitalism" (p. 90). In this instance, the argument over location authenticity is constructed as a trivial complaint made by a Hollywood labor force unaware of the globalizing nature of their industry; where the images on the screen were becoming as transnational and hybridized as the economics that supported them. This included the production crews overseas, which runaway directors and producers described as being more "authentic" than Hollywood labor because they were uncorrupted by unions, and more enthusiastic, and creative in their work. These judgments are argued to serve a disciplinary function, once again reinstating the power geometry of the global Hollywood industry and reminding Hollywood's below-the-line labor of their subordinate position to the industry's mobile elite.

A common justification for shooting on location in Europe in the postwar era focused on the changing tastes of American audiences. According to prominent producers and directors of the time, audiences were more sophisticated and well-travelled than in the past. Millions of servicemen had seen and experienced life in Europe and the Pacific nations up-close, they argued, and would settle for nothing less than cinematic realism. In a lengthy commentary in the *Hollywood Reporter*'s 1959 anniversary issue, actor Anthony Perkins,[6] warned that a return to old fashioned soundstage productions in Hollywood would not be enough to satisfy the modern movie-goer (Perkins, 1959). Once they had become accustomed to real locations in film, rather than sets on soundstages, audiences would never want to go back. Perkins further discussed the benefits of shooting in exotic locations such as Thailand, where both the actors and the audience could engage in the "realism and excitement always attendant to location filming." But in Perkins's view, this excitement was not limited to overseas productions; domestic productions such as Otto Preminger's *Anatomy of a Murder* (1959) (shot on location in Michigan) and Alfred Hitchcock's *North by Northwest* (1959) (filmed on location in Chicago, New York, and Mount Rushmore in South Dakota) had benefitted greatly from shooting outside Hollywood for the sake of location authenticity.

Other industry insiders offered their opinions on creative runaways and the types of circumstances that warranted filming outside Hollywood. The December 1960 issue of *The Journal of the Screen Producers Guild* (JSPG) was focused entirely on the question of runaway film production and location shooting, with several prominent producers providing commentary from all sides of the debate. In producer Darryl Zanuck's lively piece, "Shoot it where you find it!," he insisted that the issue of location authenticity was much more complicated than most understood it to be. He argued that creative integrity, and not economics, should be the deciding factor in shooting abroad; but at the same time, creative integrity did not always mean shooting on location. The ancient Jerusalem depicted in *The Greatest Story Ever Told*, no longer existed, so there was no reason to shoot on location. But Zanuck defended location shooting in places that were too special to be recreated due to their unique "local atmosphere," such as the Cote d'Ivoire of West Africa, or Dublin, Ireland (Zanuck, 1960, p. 3). In his final assessment, the film industry's job was to rise above "television dimensions and phony reproductions," and give audiences something they could only see in theaters (p. 31). Location authenticity, which Zanuck and many others in the industry at the time equated with geographic, racial and cultural exoticism (Shohat & Stam, 1994), was one way to accomplish that goal.

In his *JSPG* article, Kirk Douglas generally agreed with Zanuck's position on location authenticity and period films, standing behind his decision to shoot most of his "sword and sandal" epic, *Spartacus* (1960), in Hollywood rather than Rome. Like Zanuck's Jerusalem, Douglas and the other creative directors of the film agreed that the ancient Rome of the story was no longer apparent in the modern city. But as he explained in his jocular style, the decision to shoot in Hollywood wasn't without some personal sacrifice, including good food, good music, world-class museums, and "girl-pinching" (Douglas, 1960, p. 5). He accepted, however, that location shooting was sometimes necessary, as on his film *The Vikings* (1958), in which they needed locations with ancient castles and fjord-like waterways—neither of which could be found in and around Los Angeles, but were available on the coast of France. Ending with a patriotic flourish, Kirk Douglas expressed doubt that he would ever leave Hollywood again to make movies unless absolutely necessary, and declared "Hollywood is where the grass is greenest" (p. 6).

For producer William Perlberg (1960), technological improvements in movie exhibition, including Cinemascope, were a primary reason filmmakers were seeking out exotic locations overseas and shooting less in Hollywood. He agreed with Douglas and Zanuck, that scripts with historical content were often the determining factor in where and how a film would be made. But rather than contending that ancient historical settings could be recreated anywhere, he argued that recent history, specifically World War II, absolutely required location shooting. Based on his experience making the war film *The Counterfeit Traitor* (1962), it was not only the authenticity of the real locations and their remaining ruins from the war, but also the availability of other authentic set pieces, like World War II-era German train cars and tri-motor planes (p. 7). Perlberg also agreed that the local human factor was important in capturing the essence of authenticity of a place. But for his film *Traitor*, it was more about what the local technicians brought to the film than perhaps the extras in front of the camera. The technicians and set dressers hired on location had lived through the war and new its aesthetic in a way that Hollywood production workers simply couldn't.

The redundancy of Hollywood location shooting, and the incessant filming of the iconic Griffith Park in Los Angeles, became its own point of contention within the creative runaway debates. Griffith Park was well known as a "go-to" location in Hollywood, and featured prominently in the film classics *Birth of a Nation* (1915) and *Rebel Without a Cause* (1955). Director Philip Dunne (1961) challenged the language of the runaway production debate in his article "Griffith Park is not Enough," referring to a well-known Hollywood industry adage: "A tree is a tree, a rock is a rock, shoot it in Griffith Park!" Dunne argued that because he actively searched for interesting locations, he felt it was more accurate to call his projects "run-to," rather than "runaway," productions.

Producer-writer Samuel Marx recycled the "Griffith Park" allusion in his 1968 *JSPG* commentary on runaway production. But his critique of the anti-runaway lobby displayed none of the patience or subtlety of Dunne's. Rather, he chastised those opposing foreign production for location authenticity, questioning their sense of progress as well as their intelligence. The Griffith Park saying was created at a time when audiences were less sophisticated, and more easily fooled by efforts to make L.A. locations look exotic or foreign (Marx, 1968, p. 9). Marx then moved on to criticize Hollywood production labor for their rigid adherence to union wages and job descriptions, and lauding the "altruisitic" film crews overseas—where "[p]rop men plug in lights with no objections from electricians" (p. 10). In the end, he argued that in an industry that was globalizing both creatively and economically, it was labor's dogged commitment to a non-existent thing called "runaway production" that was really at the bottom of Hollywood's employment troubles. Marx's comments are perhaps the most explicit example of the disciplinary nature of the counterdiscourse to creative runaway production. Although from Marx's perspective, it is not above-the-line industry interests who are disciplining below-the-line labor through the practice of overseas "runaway" production. Rather, below-the-line labor are constructed as punishing themselves through their lack of understanding of the globalized and mobile nature of their industry.

While producers, directors, and film stars had their say about creative runaways in the trade press, Hollywood film crews made their own efforts to explicate the issue at the IATSE's 1966 convention in Detroit. Several anti-runaway film production resolutions were presented at the convention, many with a focus on so-called location authenticity productions overseas. Delegate Donald Haggarty of Burbank's Film Technicians Local 683 called attention to the trend in "spaghetti Westerns" being made in Italy and Spain, soliciting laughter from the audience when he commented, "I guess that is 'authentic locale,' because there are a lot of Italian cowboys" (IATSE, 1966, p. 194). Haggarty's resolution called for support of House Bill 6010, which condemned "unfair competition" and "deceptive" exhibition, advertising, and distribution practices related to films made outside the United States. The Bill specifically called for location labelling on such films so that audiences would be aware of where the films were made.

Along with the issue of deception in runaway productions, Haggarty was also disturbed by the borrowing of Hollywood's "authentic" identity as a production center by overseas film industries. After quoting a London paper describing their city as "Hollywood East," Haggarty complained, "Not only are they stealing the jobs of the American craftsmen and technicians, but they are bragging about it" (p. 194). Haggarty's comments drew passionate response, particularly from Delegate A. T. Dennison of Hollywood's Studio Lighting Technicians Local 728. He railed against the misrepresentation of American culture and values in films made abroad, describing how the film *The Victors* (1963), made in England by black-listed director-writer Carl Foreman, had depicted American soldiers as cruel and ruthless killers. Before being called into order by IATSE president Richard Walsh, Dennison challenged the delegation to fight for pictures that portrayed America and its people as "decent" and "respectable" (p. 196). The resolutions and statements made by the IATSE delegates clearly articulated their desire to reterritorialize their industry, both on and off the screen. For them, Hollywood and the United States were the authentic "spaces of belonging" of the motion picture industry, both geographically and rhetorically (Morley, 2001). But by all accounts, the deterritorialization and commodification of the Hollywood industry were already in full swing by 1966. Claims at being the authentic "home" to the industry, or claims that Hollywood films were the exclusive domain of American nationalism, were becoming harder to make.

And yet, creative runaway concerns were not isolated to foreign film production. In the late 1960s, industry observers noted a surge in domestic film production, with many staged outside Los Angeles for the purposes of location authenticity. Not everyone bought the explanation, including Robert Windeler of the *New York Times*. Cynically describing Hollywood as the "former film capital," he hypothesized that the "ever-blossoming" problem of domestic runaway production was likely due to cheaper labor and the availability of "sixth-day" shooting schedules in other states[7]—heavily penalized by Hollywood unions—and not location authenticity as claimed (Windeler, 1969, p. 131). New York City, a long-time production rival of Hollywood, mounted a more concerted effort to build its reputation as a major film center and attract more film work in the mid-1960s, with some apparent success (Garrigues, 1966). *Barefoot in the Park* (1967), *The Odd Couple* (1968), *The Producers* (1968), and *Rosemary's Baby* (1968) were just a few of the high-profile films from this era that prominently featured New York as their backdrop. The city's heavily unionized production community argued that both New York's unique locales and efforts to break down licensing barriers for productions, spearheaded by Mayor John Lindsay, were responsible for their boost in productions—and not "runaway" incentives or overinflated production figures as some Hollywood industry people intimated (Sutherland, 1968).

Other U.S. locations also began to market their unique attributes in an effort to attract creative runaways from Hollywood. Actor Richard Boone became a vocal advocate of a developing production community in Hawaii, arguing that the state has many of the attractive qualities of California, including beautiful weather and scenery (MacMinn, 1968, August 21, p. F21). While the TV series *Hawaii 5-0* had come to the state for realism and to take advantage of the tropical scenery, Boone contended that other film and TV genres, particularly Westerns, would find plenty of useful locations—the "big" island boasted ranches with over 40,000 head of cattle and cactus-strewn landscapes that could easily stand in for Arizona. When asked whether Hollywood labor might perceive the Hawaii production push to be a case of economic "runaway" production, Boone offered his interpretation of the difference: "After all, Hawaii is very much a part of the United States. This is not foreign production" (F21). Jack Lord, star of *Hawaii 5-0* also responded to the runaway production accusation, arguing on the basis of the impracticalities of shooting on the islands. In fact, it was costing the production company 25–30 percent more to shoot in Hawaii. But the authentic environment was worth the expense (MacMinn, 1968, August 20, p. F17). Heading off the suggestion that the TV show was there just for the luxury of living and working in Hawaii, Lord added, "We're here to work. This is not a laua."

The domestic version of the creative runaway debate finally arrived at Hollywood's backdoor, as productions staged in other parts of California came under the suspicion of Hollywood unions and industry reporters. *Los Angeles Times* writer Robert Joseph (1967) quipped that as Mayor Yorty had turned his attention to bringing runaway productions back to L.A. from far-flung locations such as Yugoslavia and Spain, other film projects were "slipping out the back door" and heading to San Francisco (p. C16). A few critically acclaimed films had come out of the northern California city in the late 1960s, including Mike Nichols' *The Graduate* (1967) and *Guess Who's Coming to Dinner?* (1967), as well as the hit TV series *Ironside* (1967). California directors like Nichols and Dick Lester (*Hard Day's Night*, 1964) justified their location choices as ones based in creativity and not economics. Speaking about his San Francisco-based production *Petulia* (1968), Lester argued that in terms of aesthetic, San Francisco was "more subtle" than Los Angeles, and for a love story, the former was preferrable (p. C16). Robert Joseph pointed out the dual ironies of Lester's *Petulia*: the first being that the production was British-funded and in some ways a runaway from Shepperton, England; the second irony was that the original novel, John Haase's *Me and the Arch Kook Petulia*, was set in Santa Monica and Hollywood, making it "a particularly bitter production pill to swallow" for the L.A. film community (p. C16).

Debates over domestic creative runaways represented a final stage in the de-territorializing of the Hollywood film industry, and the disciplining of Hollywood labor in the 1960s. The globalization of the industry had come home, and the local, authentic, spaces of belonging constructed by Hollywood labor for their industry had been violated. Just as it had been demonstrated to Hollywood labor that they were interchangable within the New International Division of Cultural Labor, it was now made plain that Hollywood, as an authentic space of production, could be deconstructed and replaced within the NICL at will; and the NICL was not only made of faraway places, but also local spaces like San Francisco, tantalizingly close to Hollywood. As Appadurai (1996) has suggested, the flow of financial capital and the construction and flow of images wthin the NICL are closely linked. And if a minor adjustment in the mediascape is needed to make capital flow more freely through the finanscape, such as the restaging of a narrative just outside Hollywood and its restrictive union rules and salary requirements, then so be it.

Domestic runaway production would become an even more prominent issue of debate in the 1970s and 1980s, as many other U.S. communities previously unaffiliated with the industry, such as Orlando, began to compete for Hollywood production dollars. Hollywood labor would once again attempt to re-territorialize their industry by building alliances with other California production communities and state agencies in an effort to construct California as the authentic home to the film production industry.

CONCLUSION

Hollywood film production underwent substantial changes in the 1960s. Most notably, the industry had to find new ways to get the attention of Baby

Boomer audiences distracted by television, and new distibution markets to offset the impact of media fragmentation on domestic box office revenues. The result was an industry that had to shift from a model of mass production in the studio era, to a much more selective production model focused on a few spectacular blockbuster films, the marketability of a handful of high-demand movie stars, and new distribution outlets at home and abroad. Discussions of runaway production in this time underwent a parallel shift, critiquing the dubious explanations offered by producers for filming outside Hollywood, including the argument that Hollywood labor would ultimately benefit from investments in production abroad. And yet, this is a familiar pattern that has been observed across globalizing industries dependent on large, manual labor forces. Manufacturers divest themselves of as much of the expenses of production as possible, outsourcing the work to the lowest global bidder. At the same time, such companies shift their investments to the more lucrative distribution process, promising that the revenues generated from expanding overseas markets will create more work on the domestic front. Christopherson & Storper (1989) describe this development as a shift from media industries that were vertically organized in the studio era, to ones that are now horizontally organized through the concentration of media ownership and oligopoly. In the studio era, Hollywood majors invested in all parts of the process—from development, to production, to exhibition. But in the industry that was evolving in the 1960s, the old studios were becoming media corporations, horizontally invested across media industries and national boundaries.

What makes the film industry's evolution toward horizontal integration unique is the fact that the product being made was so deeply situated in culture and place. And in the 1960s, both labor and producers used these unique characteristics to support their arguments for domestic versus overseas production. For producers and Hollywood's industry elite, the new emphasis on exotic, spectacle films was a matter of fiscal necessity—a response to changing tastes and lifestyles. The fact that films such as *Cleopatra* and *Spartacus* often required overseas locations, either for authenticity's sake or for much-needed access to human or infrastructural resources, was incidental and not an intentional "running away" from Hollywood's production community, or so producers claimed. For Hollywood labor, however, the push for location authenticity and large-scale, blockbuster productions too-conveniently served the social and economic motives of Hollywood's producers and stars. Rather, location authenticity and blockbuster productions were seen as newly-conceived excuses to perpetuate runaway production practices set in motion in the 1940s and 1950s by frozen funds and tax exempton policies, including the use of generous foreign subsidies, the hiring of cheap, non-union "atmosphere," and the indulgence in extravagant lifestyles by Hollywood's elite talent.

In addition to shifts in creative and economic contructions of runaway film production, there were also changes in the political landscape of the runaway production debates in the 1960s. In the previous two decades, Hollywood labor's power to influence production practices, at home and abroad, had been predicated on their ability to conjure the forces of Americanism engendered during World War II. But as the war faded into history and patriotism took a backseat to emerging, lucrative trade relationships with Europe, Hollywood film labor's construction of runaway film production as un-Americanism began to fall apart. With the end of the blacklist in the 1960s, officially recognized with the crediting of screenwriter Dalton Trumbo on one of Hollywood's most successful blockbusters, *Spartacus* (1960), the film industry's above-the-liners were able to turn the tables on Hollywood labor, portraying so-called runaway productions as the salvation of a domestic industry damaged by labor's anti-communist crusades. Hollywood's below-the-line labor was rapidly losing ground in their struggles against runaway film production, while Hollywood's jet-setting elite seemed to continually gain political and economic capital within the New International Division of Cultural Labor. This is consistent with Massey's (1994) description of the power geometry within the international division of labor as a self-perpetuating force. The more control that Hollywood's above-the-line interests could gain over the construction and flow of the political, economic, and aesthetic "scapes" of the globalizing film industry, the less power that below-the-line labor had over them.

By the end of the 1960s, the labor groups that had been so effective in organizing and defining Hollywood's anti-runaway production movement, particularly the AFL Film Council and the IATSE, were almost completely absent from the discourse. In the future, below-the-line labor would need to relaunch their efforts to recruit allies better situated within the power geometry of the NICL—namely policy makers who might be able to reconstruct the "finanscape" of California and redirect the flow of runaway productions back to Hollywood on behalf of labor.

NOTES

1. Thomas M. Pryor covered the film industry for the *New York Times* for thirty years before joining *Daily Variety* as its chief editor in 1959. He remained at *Variety* until his retirement in 1988. Given his long tenure with each publication and his regular attention to the issue of runaway production, it is important to note the crucial

role that Pryor played in framing the issue in the American press during the twentieth century.

2. Preminger has been identified by some as the first to defy the Hollywood "blacklist" by hiring Dalton Trumbo to write the screenplay for his 1960 release *Exodus* (Weiler, 1960).

3. According to Bernstein's (1957) report, the average below-the-line film worker made around $3 an hour in 1957, about $0.30 per hour less than a construction worker with a comparable job title (e.g., painter, electrician, Teamster) (p. 40).

4. Color television was not widely adopted in the United States until the late 1960s, when the major networks began to broadcast most of their line-ups in color (http://www.fcc.gov/cgb/kidszone/history_colortv.html).

5. Calculating for inflation, this would be the equivalent of roughly $360 million in 2015 U.S. currency.

6. Anthony Perkins made a string of films in Europe throughout the 1960s and 1970s, including *Goodbye Again* (France, 1961), *Five Miles to Midnight* (France, 1962), *Phaedra* (Greece, 1962), *Is Paris Burning?* (France, 1966), and *Ten Days of Wonder* (France, 1971).

7. Union pay rates are predicated on a five-day shooting schedule. If a shooting schedule goes to a sixth consecutive day of shooting, union film workers start the day in overtime.

Chapter Three

Running Ink

Offshore Animation and the Rise of Domestic Runaway Production

Major U.S. news outlets devoted considerably less time to the subject of runaway production in the 1970s and 1980s. Even the *Los Angeles Times*, which no doubt served the largest population of readers concerned with the issue, published only sixty stories directly referencing runaway production in the 1970s and 1980s combined, compared to seventy-one stories in the 1960s alone. Puette (1992) argued in minute detail that the 1970s and 1980s were a time when news media coverage of organized labor was in flux. Print and TV news were becoming more consolidated and corporatized in this time, leading to intensifying hostility between media owners and the many unions and guilds that populated the news industry. Subsequently, Puette suggests that corporate interests began to exercise more editorial control over the inclusion, placement, and framing of labor stories in the press, with the overall effect of marginalizing and demonizing unions in the news. In short, a commercially-driven news media was becoming more concerned with selling news than serving the public interest, and reporting on the causes of union disputes was simply less newsworthy—and less profitable—than the news which considered the possible effects and inconveniences for their readers. And given that the inconveniences created by runaway production primarily impacted Hollywood labor, and not media audiences, the issue was beginning to fall off the agenda of the major mass media.

Despite diminishing knowledge or interest in runaway production among the public, the issue remained an active subject within the Hollywood production industry. Trade press outlets, like *Variety* and *The Hollywood Reporter*, continued documenting important shifts in legislative strategies, production practices, and perspectives on union culpability in regard to California's ever-unstable film industry. The most significant among these shifts were an increased concern with domestic runaway production, foreign competition for television work, and the exportation of production services such as animation and film lab processing to other countries. The 1970s and 1980s also marked a time of growing awareness of the runaway potential of Canada and Mexico—countries whose borders with the United States delineated highly divergent attitudes and policies toward labor management, film industry subsidies, and the free trade of cultural commodities.

The shift in the discourse toward domestic competition in the 1970s and 1980s is argued to coincide with a new stage of re-territorialization of the Hollywood film industry that emphasized localism and regionalism over nationalism. But this is not to say that the development of regional competition and a discourse of domestic runaway film production were separate phenomena from the development of global Hollywood. Rather, as Pieterse (2004) has noted, globalization is more than an internationalizing of capitalist systems of production, distribution, and consumption, but instead involves an "*increase in the available modes of organization:* transnational, international, macro-regional, national, micro-regional, municipal, local" (p. 50, emphasis in the original). Though there had been some scattered mentions of domestic runaway production problems in previous decades, most of the early debates were focused on foreign competition and the role of the nation-state in regulating transnational production and trade relationships. And indeed, many of Hollywood's anti-runaway production policy efforts up through the 1960s put great emphasis on garnering support from federal legislators for national-level tariffs and trade embargoes. In the 1970s and 1980s, however, below-the-line production labor joined forces with municipal and state agencies of business and tourism to form film offices dedicated to creating industry-friendly policies to attract runaway productions, or in the case of California and Hollywood, to bring such productions "home." The resulting discourse of domestic runaway film production appears to reflect this growing interconnection between municipal, state, regional, and transnational processes within the globalizing film industry, and the ease with which Hollywood's media corporations navigated labor policy and coordinated production processes across these multiple planes.

A second, closely related theme that emerges is the role of new media and communication technologies in facilitating transnational media production and labor outsourcing. These were decades of rapid advancement in computer and telecommunications technologies, and media production industries, like many others, were quick to utilize these tools to reduce costs and speed production. Within discussions of runaway film production, Hollywood labor lamented the impact of technological development on jobs previously considered safe from exportation, including editing, special effects, and animation work. Some discussions of runaway film production during this time also seem to anticipate the role that networked communications would play in facilitating runaway productions: allowing producers to easily manage several worksites from one central location, or to electronically outsource high-tech production services such as special effects. In this way, the evolution of runaway production in the 1970s and 1980s signals a crucial stage in Hollywood's development into a global "media capital": a creative and financial industry hub "bound up in a web of relations that exist at the local, regional and global levels, as well as the national level" and managed through rapidly developing new media and communications technologies (Curtin, 2003, p. 204; Schiller, 2000).

RUNAWAY TELEVISION PRODUCTION

The 1970s and 1980s marked a time of heightened interdependence and convergence between television and film industries. The rise in popularity of cable television and premium movie channels like HBO in the mid 1970s provided a powerful new distribution outlet for both old and new Hollywood films. The sudden growth in television channels via cable also meant an increased demand for original content, including made-for-TV movies and cable-exclusive television series (Mullen, 2008). Likewise, the introduction of the videocassette recorder in the late 1970s, at first seen by Hollywood film interests as a "subversive" technology and the inevitable downfall of their industry, was fully embraced in the 1980s as an equally valuable distribution outlet and lucrative revenue stream (Wasser, 2001).

Overall, where the growth of the Hollywood film industry had seemed to stagnate over the previous two decades, the television industry had continued to expand and flourish. And in the end, it could be argued that the television and film industries needed each other to survive—the former with limitless distribution potential, the latter with limitless content production capabilities. It was then, perhaps, inevitable that Hollywood producers would begin to look to foreign markets for budget-friendly television production locations, just as they had done in the past for film productions; and equally inevitable that foreign competition for television production would make its way into the runaway production debates of the 1970s and 1980s.

In the 1970 anniversary issue of *Variety*, Hollywood Film Council president John Lehners identified runaway production as film labor's number one concern for twenty years running (Lehners, 1970). Among the seven factors Lehners outlined as contributing to runaway production and Hollywood unemployment, changes in television production practices accounted for three:

specifically, the export of television production work and financing to foreign locations, the reduction of episodic TV schedules, and the increase in rerun television programming.

Foreign economic runaway production had always been a core concern for U.S. film labor leaders, and naturally carried over into the runaway television debates. What labor didn't anticipate was that foreign competition for television production might come from the noncommercial sector of public television. In 1970, the Mobil Corporation issued a much-publicized $1.1 million grant to the Corporation for Public Broadcasting, of which roughly half was allocated to underwrite thirty-nine one-hour episodes of the British-made series *Masterpiece Theater*, including its distribution to U.S. audiences by public television station WGBH Boston (Gould, 1970). The move was denounced by IATSE representatives as a blatant act of runaway investment, with American dollars supporting the British film industry at the expense of American jobs. When it was discovered that the Motion Picture Pension Fund—representing 38 unions and guilds, 27,000 production workers, and $99 million in investments—included 21,000 shares of Mobil stock, the fund's chairman, Donald Haggerty, threatened to dump the stock and stage boycotts, rallies, and picket lines in retaliation for the company's disloyalty to the U.S. industry. IATSE members were even encouraged to get rid of their Mobil credit cards, with Haggerty proclaiming, "We're going to tear a page out of Cesar Chavez's book" (Steiger, 1970, p. D11).

In his article on the Mobil incident, *New York Times* columnist Jack Gould considered whether the educational goals of public television outweighed the "runaway" investment concerns of the U.S. production unions. His final comments suggested sympathy for the former when he observed, "If various forms of TV can narrow cultural breaches and promote social and economic understanding, particularly in times of stress, they should be given free reign to do so" (Gould, 1970, p. 123). Gould's comments reflect the contradictory political rationality of public TV, in which reasoned debate among an educated white citizenry was prioritized over the supposedly irrational and emotional social dilemmas raised by the less educated working class, including union labor (Ouellette, 2002). In this instance, public television's mission to bring quality, educational programming to the U.S. masses, even at the expense of U.S. labor, was a price worth paying. Mobil executives called the whole situation "an unfortunate misunderstanding," explaining to the unions that the company had merely purchased rights to older programming, which had already been produced and aired in England. The Mobil execs also contended that introducing American audiences to the theater-style programming of the *Masterpiece* series might create future demand for similar productions in the United States.

While it appears that Donald Haggerty conceded to the agenda of the oil giant, his intentions for an anti-runaway production rally were still realized. On November 30, 1970, more than 3,000 union film workers attended an anti-runaway production rally at the Los Angeles Palladium, sponsored by the Hollywood Film Council (Wright, 1970). Council president John Lehners was flanked by some of the industry's most avid legislative supporters, including Pennsylvania Representative John H. Dent (D-PA), Senator-elect John Tunney (D-CA), and California Governor and long-time anti-runaway production campaigner Ronald Reagan. Dent, who had served as chairman of the Education and Labor subcommittee on Imports and Exports during the 1961 Washington hearings on runaway production, promised rally attendees that he would hold a new round of hearings on the issue. Tunney and Reagan both proposed a 20 percent tax incentive package for films made in the United States, as well as the possible need for tariffs on imports. For Reagan, a U.S. film industry subsidy could be justified, if only as a token of appreciation for the industry's cultural and economic service to its country, and not as an economic life preserver. While acknowledging the merits of Dent and Reagan's diplomatic approach to the film industry's unemployment problems, Lehners suggested stronger measures were needed to get their point across to runaway producers. He read a letter of support from the leadership of the AFL-CIO offering to back any film union boycotts or "concerted trade union economic activities" organized against runaway productions (p. 84). The planned boycotts would not only target runaway motion pictures, but also American products depicted in runaway commercials, a growing trend according to Lehners.

Some of the anti-runaway initiatives and counter-actions proposed at the Palladium rally managed to gain some traction following the event. A tax-related Domestic Film Production Incentive Act outlining the 20 percent tax rebate program endorsed by Reagan and Dent was introduced to Congress by Representative James Corman (D-CA) in spring of 1971 (Dales, 1971). Twenty-six industry leaders, including IATSE's Richard Walsh and the MPAA's Jack Valenti, attended a two-hour meeting with President Nixon to discuss the incentive bill. Also on the agenda were industry concerns regarding the Federal Communications Commission's 1970 Financial Interest and Syndication Rules, which restricted the amount of network programming that network owned and affiliated stations could carry during primetime to encourage more local and independent programming (Lotz, 2007). Hollywood labor feared the Access Rule would further suppress production schedules in an already anemic employment climate. Nixon, however, described the tax incentive bill as a "Pandora's Box" that the executive office was not willing to open during the present Congressional session (Nixon Nixes Hollywood Relief, 1971). He also washed his hands of the Access Rule issue, pointing out that the FCC was an independent agency and subsequently out of his jurisdiction. Industry interests continued to press Nixon for legislative support for the U.S. film industry over the next few years, with Ronald Reagan having reportedly sent a personal letter to the president in fall of 1971 urging his consideration of yet another tax incentive bill proposed by the Joint Labor-Management Committee for Domestic Motion Picture Production (Gov. Reagan wants Nixon's Aid, 1971). As with previous efforts, this bill was also met with apathy by the Nixon White House.

Television had provided additional demands for production work beyond programming, namely the lucrative market of commercial production. In 1976 alone, advertisers spent $5.9 billion on television advertising to reach the 69 million American households that watched an average of 6 hours of TV a day (*History: 1970s*, 2003, September 15). However, in spring 1972, the trade press reported a distinct trend in Hollywood production companies setting up branches in Mexico specifically for making commercials. One such company, Cinemobile, had produced a Canadian Beer commercial in Churubusco Studios just outside Mexico City, a move that had saved the company $24,000 in production costs (Tusher, 1972). But the real incentive seemed to be the savings generated from the use of Mexican, non-SAG actors. By avoiding the American guild, Cinemobile estimated they would skirt $17,000 per year in residuals payments for a commercial slated for a three-year run. And because the actors were bilingual, the commercial was shot in both English and Spanish, allowing for broader distribution of the spot.

Incensed by the blatant runaway activities of companies like Cinemobile, several film labor groups organized a protest march against runaway commercial production on October 27, 1972 in New York City. Six hundred people representing twelve unions within the East Coast Council of IATSE and the Conference of Motion Picture and Television Unions paraded down Madison Avenue, holding up banners with the slogan, "If you show it in America, if you sell it in America, make it in America" (Dougherty, 1972; Fighting Runaway Production, 1972–73). Many journalists at the event cited one of the highlights of the day as the inclusion of a camera crane mounted on the back of a truck, straddled by a beautiful woman carrying a sign that read, "Make it with me in America."

At a rally in Grand Army Plaza following the march, industry officials, including Grand Marshall and IATSE president Richard Walsh, blamed overseas production and domestic non-union production of television commercials for approximately $3.5 million in lost wages for U.S. workers (Dougherty, 1972, p. 50). Other trade union leaders urged their members to boycott products made by runaway advertisers; most notably, toy manufacturers were singled out as producing their commercials "on a runaway scale." The crowd was also urged to throw their support behind the Foreign Trade and Investment Act of 1972—also known as the Burke-Hartke Trade Bill—sponsored by Representative James Burke (D-MA) and Senator Vance Hartke (D-IN). The bill outlined a general plan for restricting imports in all sectors of the economy, including the creation of a federal commission that would establish annual production schedules and import quotas. It also proposed to impose some control over the "geographic patterns of goods" (Canto, 1983/84), which made it particularly compatible with the film and television industries' efforts to retain more production within Hollywood and the United States more generally. Though the Burke-Hartke Bill never passed, it was considered highly influential in setting a protectionist tone for subsequent industry and trade discussions in the years to come.

Though legislative efforts continued to be frustrated, a few television producers responded proactively to labor's protests against runaway production. In 1971, the popular series *Bewitched* had planned to shoot eight episodes in Europe as part of a family vacation storyline (Bewitched Remains H'wood, 1971). However, producer William Asher decided to shoot the episodes in Southern California instead, explaining that, "No producer today can morally afford to take his show out of Hollywood. The employment crisis in Hollywood is such that we must call upon our ingenuity to keep all production at home" (p. 1). Asher conceded that the show had travelled to Salem, Massachusetts the previous year to shoot eight special episodes—the location being particularly relevant to the show's witchcraft theme. The difference for Asher in the case of the Salem shoot was that the entire Hollywood crew had been flown to the East Coast for the occasion, which would not have been the case had the show decided to shoot its European episodes overseas. Asher additionally attempted to bolster his reputation as a nonrunaway producer by pointing out that he kept the primary production of *Bewitched* in Hollywood, even though the family depicted in the show was supposed to live in Westport, Connecticut.

Discussions of runaway television production took a notable turn in the 1980s, with increasingly frequent mentions of competition from Canada. While Canadian runaway production will be discussed in greater detail in the following chapter, it is worth noting here that some of the earliest mentions of Canadian runaway production in the U.S. press involved the production of television series and "movies of the week" (aka MOWs). In an article describing the "cut-rate" Canadian TV trend, Morgan Gendel (1986) of the *Los Angeles Times* outlined several economic incentives drawing Hollywood producers to Vancouver and Toronto, including a favorable exchange rate of CDN$1.38 to one US$1, anywhere from $15,000 to $65,000 in monthly savings on studio space rental over Los Angeles, the ability to use IATSE affiliated crews, and the ability to negotiate a one-time residuals buyout with Canadian actors (represented by the Alliance of Canadian Cinema, Television and Radio Artists), saving producers roughly 50 percent over what they would normally pay American Screen Actors Guild members (pp. SD–D1). Even with airfares and per diem costs figured in for necessary U.S. talent and crew, one producer estimated that savings were still around 20 percent to 25 percent for most productions.

Though Canadian runaway production created concern for Hollywood labor, the quality of the productions was generally derided in the U.S. press. Gendel noted that U.S. primetime TV producers would "snicker" at the common use of 16-millimeter film on Canadian productions—a choice that was made to save money on film stock, but not without implications for image quality. The trials and tribulations of a movie-of-the-week called *Firefighter*, depicting the story of the first female firefighter hired by the Los Angeles fire department, were also described with some amusement by U.S. film industry commentators: the production had suffered near-constant rain showers and water-stained wardrobe while on location in Vancouver (Wilson, 1986); another reviewer noted that neither the script nor the scenery "rang true," calling *Firefighter* the "ultimate runaway production" for filming the Los Angeles story in Vancouver (Margulies, 1986, p. G10). But not all Canadian productions could be so easily criticized, with successful television series such as *Night Heat* (1985–1989) paving the way for the tremendous rise in quality film and television productions that would come out of Canada in the 1990s and 2000s.

The discourse of runaway television production rehashed many of the themes used in past debates, including runaway foreign investment and, to a certain extent, runaway un-Americanism as it appeared within the "buy American, film American" discourse concerning commercial runaways. A unique characteristic of the 1970s anti-runaway television debates, however, was the much more visible, activist approach taken by labor in the staging of large-scale rallies. The "protest march" strategy could certainly be attributed to the times, when anti-Vietnam War protests and pro-ERA marches were common occurrences. But much like anti-war and women's rights activism in the 1960s and 1970s (Gitlin, 1980; Tuchman, 1978), labor's anti-runaway rallies received little coverage or positive support in the popular press. But when they did receive attention from the press, the emphasis was put on the appearance of celebrity participants rather than a serious discussion of the issues.

It also seems evident that the issue of runaway television production was beginning to garner some local and regional appeal, spurring production communities and legislators outside Hollywood and California to get involved in a way not necessarily seen in previous runaway film production efforts.

This may be attributable to the more localized nature of television compared to film, in that TV plays a more crucial role in the construction of localized community identities and the circulation of local and regional values (Morley & Robins, 1995). While the film industry "belonged" to Hollywood, the television industry belonged to all American communities, big and small, who relied on the medium for local news and local-interest programming. And as a more community-based medium, it would have been much easier for members of Congress and state politicians to throw their support behind anti-runaway television production initiatives because they could argue the importance of such legislation to the maintenance of their local economies and cultures.

The loss of television production to runaway practices would continue to be a concern for U.S. labor, though the damage was generally limited to short-schedule, smaller budget productions such as commercials and movies-of-the-week. By contrast, major television series tended to remain in New York and Hollywood for the simple fact that television stars and core production staff chafed at the idea of living in far-flung locations for extended periods of time, perhaps years if a show was successful. But even this obstacle would be challenged in years to come when TV series began to set up shop in Vancouver, B.C.—a mere two-and-a-half hour flight from Los Angeles.

ANIMATION AND THE RUNAWAY WARS

Until the 1970s, discussions of runaway film production had stayed relatively focused on location-based production, such as live-action feature films. Beginning in the 1970s, however, other sectors of the industry that had seemed impervious to outsourcing trends began to surface within the runaway debates, including animation.

Animation had been a part of the Hollywood film industry almost as long as the industry had resided in Southern California, with Walt Disney Studios serving as its anchor since the 1920s (Wasko, 2001). The animation industry grew along with the demand for animated features, and in 1941, animation workers chartered the Screen Cartoon Guild Local 852 with the help of union leader Herb Sorrell. The Cartoon Guild, however, was short-lived, having been broken up by Roy Brewer in 1947 in his efforts to dismantle Sorrell's Conference of Studio Unions (CSU); in 1952, the Hollywood cartoonists re-organized as IATSE Local 839, though they continued to be recognized as an independent guild. Hollywood and New York animators managed to skirt the runaway production turmoil experienced by the movie and television unions in the 1950s and 1960s, mostly due to the specialized nature of the work and the concentration of skilled animators in the United States. But in the early 1970s, the increasing demand for cable television content sent Hollywood animation studios in search of inexpensive workers, particularly for the labor-intensive ink and paint portion of production (Wells, 2003). Australia, Japan, South Korea, Taiwan, and the Philippines were all prime locations for the outsourcing of Hollywood animation work (Yoon & Malecki, 2009), and thus the primary focus in what would become known within the Cartoonist Guild as the "runaway wars."

On one level, labor outsourcing experienced by the animation industry in the 1970s and 1980s is easily understood as part of similar outsourcing trends that occurred within other information industries at the time, including the mass relocation of IT call centers to India (Mosco, 2006). As such, it could be argued that the outsourcing of animation production work and the subsequent debates over runaway animation support Braverman's (1974) thesis on the development of a new division of information and service labor, in which IT and service work would eventually become "de-skilled" and divided in the same way that had occurred in manufacturing. More specifically, this theory predicted that "conception" work (such as scripting and art direction) would become concentrated in an industry hub such as Hollywood, and "execution" work (such as ink and paint) would be outsourced to the lowest bidder (Mosco, 2006, p. 773). In the case of Hollywood and the animation industry, such an arrangement helped to reinforce the New International Division of Cultural Labor and the subordinate role of production labor to the more powerful producers and managers residing above-the-line.

Problems began in 1971 when Hanna-Barbera started to send "prematerials" produced by Hollywood animators to their Australian facility for completion (Ornstein, 1971). Once members of IATSE Local 839 learned of the practice, they refused to work on the projects intended for outsourcing. In a strongly worded statement to the *Hollywood Reporter*, representatives from the Cartoonists Guild explained their opposition: "The runaway production scheme is a rope around our necks and we will not put our heads into it to get management out of a bad situation at the expense of our jobs" (p. 1). Hanna-Barbera's producers called the union's threatened work stoppage a breach of contract and promised to fire anyone who refused to work on an assigned project. But in fact, the Cartoonist Guild had organized a similar—and successful—work stoppage against the children's program *Curiosity Shop*, forcing the show's producers to discontinue outsourcing completion work to Yugoslavia. A temporary resolution was eventually reached in the 1971 Hanna-Barbera case. But tensions over runaway production were rekindled eight years later when animation outsourcing became a sticking point during contract negotiations between Local 839 and Hollywood's most prominent TV animation production studios (Waters, 1979).

Hanna-Barbera, Ruby Spears Productions, and De Patie-Freleng Enterprises, producers of most of network TV's Saturday morning cartoons at the time, were accused of sending as much as 75 percent of their animation production work overseas, primarily to Taiwan, Korea, Spain, and Australia (Waters, 1979, p. A20). Production company reps countered that L.A.'s labor base was not sufficient to meet their production needs, and that they were occasionally forced to outsource work due to last-minute scheduling decisions made by the networks. While the cartoonists conceded that unpredictable network deadlines were exacerbating the problem, they felt that animation producers were more often running away to overseas production centers for economic reasons. To support their argument, they quoted producers who had openly admitted that outsourcing cut their production costs in half compared to Hollywood. In response, the cartoonists wanted to include an "anti-runaway clause" in their new three-year contract, obligating the producers to exhaust animation labor resources within Hollywood's "studio zone" before sending excess work overseas.

Producers from Hanna Barbera, Patie-Freleng, and Ruby Spears were at first eager to negotiate, as their September 8 season start date loomed. However, contract talks with the cartoonists stalled, and on August 12, 1979, 1,200 animators from IATSE Local 839 walked out of negotiations and declared a strike against the three production companies (Waters & Bernstein, 1979). Almost immediately, the animators found themselves at odds with the IATSE's international office in New York and its president, Walter Diehl, who claimed that the cartoonists' strike was unauthorized by the parent union (Bernstein, 1979). Diehl was apparently concerned that the animation strike over runaway production would interfere with plans for an industry-wide IATSE strike of all 26,000 national members over increases in wages and benefits, slated to begin around September 5. Bud Hester, president of IATSE Local 839, declined to end the animators' strike, explaining the precariousness of his situation: "If I tried to call off the strike, I'd be shot at sunrise" (p. B30). Hester also challenged Walter Diehl's claim that the animators' strike was unauthorized, countering that Diehl had given Local 839 written permission for the strike vote and verbal permission for the strike itself.

In the end, Hester's defiance of Diehl and the parent union paid off. On August 24, 1979, Ruby Spears gave in to Local 839's demands and negotiated a new contract that included the "anti-runaway clause" (Townsend, 1979). Similar agreements with Hanna Barbera and Patie-Freleng quickly followed. Local 839's vice president, Morris "Moe" Gollub, declared the foreign labor clause the first of its kind to be written into a film or television industry contract in the United States. Though initially irked by the timing of the cartoonists' strike and its possible impact on the organization of a general IATSE strike, Walter Diehl immediately coopted their anti-runaway production clause, including it in the industry-wide contract negotiations. But unlike Local 839, the IATSE international board ceded the runaway clause before the final contract was drafted.

Despite the animators' victory in 1979, enforcement of the anti-runaway clause proved difficult. Local 839 president Bud Hester accused the production companies of "blatantly violating the clause," and threatened arbitration to make the producers honor their contract (Waters, 1980). The production companies continued to paint themselves as victims of late scheduling by the studios, arguing the necessity to outsource large amounts of work in order to meet network deadlines. With the expiration of the 1979 contract looming, 1,600 union cartoonists once again walked off the job on August 5, 1982. This time they wanted a guarantee that the major production companies, including Disney, Warner Brothers, and Filmation, would honor the original 1979 agreement to give U.S. animators "first crack at the jobs" before outsourcing animation work to foreign production centers. The animation producers offered to either include the anti-runaway production clause in the new contract or negotiate wages and benefits increases for the cartoonists, but not both (Bernstein, 1982, p. E1). After nine-and-a-half weeks off the job, representatives from the IA national office stepped in and made the choice for them: as part of national IATSE contract, the cartoonists forfeited the anti-runaway production clause for a 26.2 percent pay increase, applicable to all 24,000 members of the parent union (Cartoonists End 9-1/2-Week Strike, 1982). The IA's capitulation marked the end of the "runaway wars" for Local 839.

Over the next few years, the animation industry experienced a rapid expansion: the massive growth of cable TV combined with an increasing interest in cartoons as marketing tools for the toy industry had pumped up cartoon programming from three to four hours a day in the early 1980s, to eleven-and-a-half hours per weekday by 1988 (Culhane, 1987, p. H31). And yet 47 percent of Hollywood's animators were reportedly unemployed in December 1987, with the blame once again placed on foreign runaway production practices. In a story previewing the 1988 TV animation season, Michael Webster, vice president of Disney Pictures' television animation division, defended the need for Hollywood's animation producers to outsource work, particularly to Japan: with a greenlight to create thirty hours of their new hit children's series *Duck Tales*, and a production schedule of approximately twenty weeks to produce each half-hour program for the series, Webster argued that Disney had no choice but to outsource some of the work—there just weren't enough animators in Hollywood to get the job done. Rather, he described Disney's production process as an "international work exchange," with character designs and models, soundtracks, background designs, and animation direction all done in California, while 1,500 Japanese workers were responsible for inking, painting, and photographing the completed animation cells. Though Webster admitted the outsourced work amounted to a substantial per episode savings over using U.S. animators, up to 30 percent, or $125,000 per thirty-minute program, he insisted that the primary reason for using Japanese labor was the availability of a large and highly skilled workforce (p. H33).

Criticism of the foreign animation production trend in the late 1980s, however, came from several directions, including Hollywood's animation union, domestic animation studios, and children's programming advocacy groups. Bud Hester of the Cartoonists Guild could think of no other reason for the high levels of unemployment among Hollywood animators except runaway production: "There is more animation being done today than there's ever been in history, yet we're getting a smaller piece of the action" (Culhane, 1987, p. H33). Bill Melendez, producer of Charles Schultz's *Peanuts* TV specials since the 1950s, agreed with Hester, arguing that outsourcing systems like Disney's were motivated by pure greed. Peggy Charan of the advocacy group Action for Children's Television saw the issue of animation outsourcing as intertwined with a general loss in quality of children's animated programming. But for Charan, the problem did not begin with the animation studios, but with toy manufacturers who she argued had taken over and ruined children's programming. Because of their massive investments in animation as a marketing tool for their products, toy companies were argued to have an inordinate degree of influence over content development as well as production decisions, including the use of cheap labor abroad rather than quality union labor in the United States. (p. H31).

But the possibilities for the animation industry, and the problems of runaway production, extended well beyond the children's market. In December 1989, the landscape of television animation changed forever with the debut of the longest-running and most successful "adult" animation series of all time—*The Simpsons*. After the series' first season, the bulk of its ink and paint work and "in betweens"[1] production were outsourced to South Korea, which *Simpsons* producers defended as both a matter of practicality and a matter of creative quality control (Alum Silverman Directs "Simpsons Movie," 2007; Loeb, 2007). In the true irreverent spirit of *The Simpsons*, the show's writers were willing to lampoon growing public panic over labor outsourcing, with episodes such as "Kiss Kiss, Bang Bangalore" (April 9, 2006), depicting the relocation of Springfield's nuclear power plant to India. The show's creators were also not averse to parodying their own outsourcing of labor by including a scene in the episode *Itchy and Scratchy: The Movie* (1992, November 3) in which Korean animators are seen bent over their desks, laboring away on animation cells. The monumental success of *The Simpsons* at the end of the 1980s, and the subsequent normalization of animation outsourcing, appears to have sounded the death knell for small U.S. animation studios such as Filmation that were trying to function outside the runaway foreign production model. In 1989, Filmation folded after a three-decade run of producing successful series such as *Fat Albert and the Cosby Kids* (1972) and *The Tom and Jerry Comedy Show* (1980) (Sito, 2006).

Vast changes in production technologies were also on the horizon for the animation industry, with the commercial transition to digital ink and paint work beginning in the late 1980s. Disney began to integrate computer-animated elements into their feature films in 1989,[2] and by 1995 had formed a lucrative partnership with Pixar Animation Studios to produce full-length 3D computer animated features; technology they debuted in the wildly popular film *Toy Story* (1995). Many within the Hollywood animation industry have argued that the digitizing of the production process has actually brought about a reverse runaway trend and a "Second Golden Age" for Hollywood animation in the 1990s and 2000s. Because of the concentration of high tech animation studios in Hollywood, animators there have been able to re-territorialize the industry and reestablish Hollywood's claim of being the authentic home of animation production.[3] But as Appadurai (1996) has argued, the "technoscape" of transnational media is a fluid configuration, able to quickly shift to take advantage of newly emerging political and economic incentives. As such, it is likely only a matter of time before animation laborers overseas are re-skilled for digital production, and a new cycle of runaway animation "wars" begins.

In actuality, unemployment complaints by Hollywood animation labor in the 1970s and 1980s did not only reside with foreign runaway production practices. Beginning in the early 1970s, Disney, along with several other Hollywood production interests, started to invest in production facilities in other parts of the United States, resulting in the final runaway discourse to be discussed in this chapter—domestic runaway production.

DOMESTIC RUNAWAY PRODUCTION

The 1970s and 1980s were a time when several U.S. states not traditionally associated with film production began to aggressively market themselves to Hollywood producers as amenable production locations: from billboards lining Sunset Strip declaring Illinois the place where "Show Business is Our Life," to splashy half-page ads in *The Hollywood Reporter* depicting the word "Florida"—and not Hollywood—as the iconic sign in the hills. As in the case of foreign runaway production in previous decades, the Hollywood unions questioned many of the economic incentives used to attract production to other states, including the availability of non-union workers under "right-to-work" laws, and access to state-level tax incentives. In the 1970s and 1980s, however, Hollywood unions began to work closely with California state legislators, including Governor Ronald Reagan, to make the motion picture industry a political and economic priority for the state: through numerous tax relief proposals, the creation of a state-commissioned Motion Picture Council, and high-profile hearings on California's domestic runaway production problems.

The discursive shift toward domestic runaway production is significant in that it brings to light the importance of local and regional divisions of labor and production within processes of globalization. In more traditional understandings of the political economy of globalization, the argument is often made that corporate transnationalism primarily occurs at the level of the nation-state, with local and regional interests affected mostly as an indirect result of national policies. Contemporary theories of globalization argue the diminishing importance of the nation-state to transnational industry, and specifically transnational media industries. As LeFebvre (1991) has stated, "No space disappears in the course of growth and development: the worldwide does not abolish the local" (p. 86). And in matters of production and consumption, media industries are more often operating within and between several spatial planes including, but not limited to, municipal, local, regional, national, and international domains (Christopherson, 2005; Pieterse, 2004). The development of municipal and state production communities across the United States in the 1970s and 1980s, and the domestic runaway production debates that followed, serve as evidence of the latter, multi-level construction of globalization. The rise of domestic production outside Hollywood was not a separate development from foreign production practices. As will be shown, many of the same types of production practices implemented at the international level and protested by Hollywood labor in the past were simply downsized and reapplied at the regional, state, and municipal levels in the 1970s and 1980s. The result was rather frenetic efforts by Hollywood labor to construct their problems with production outsourcing as significant to multiple political and economic interests: business and political leaders in Los Angeles, California state legislators in Sacramento, as well as federal legislators in Washington, D.C.

The issue of location authenticity, first introduced in the 1950s and 1960s, reemerges within the debates over domestic runaway production. In the 1970s and 1980s, authenticity is implemented as both a re-territorializing discourse by Hollywood labor trying to lure productions back to California, and as a de-territorializing discourse by "runaway" producers, directors, and production companies attempting to establish new production communities in other states. This again is argued to support the conceptualization of a multi-leveled, overlapping model of globalization, where the "mediascape" in which images of the world are produced, is similarly contested across local, regional, national, and international planes (Appadurai, 1996).

Georgia was among the first states to make a serious play for Hollywood production, led by Governor Jimmy Carter. The state welcomed John Boorman's *Deliverance* in 1972, granting access to the remote mountain county of Rabun, situated on the Chattooga River where much of the movie's action takes place. The production spent roughly $1 million hiring local carpenters and truck drivers, eating in local restaurants, and buying various goods and services from local shops—everything from "shoe laces to liquor" (Funke, 1974, p. 135). What the residents of Rabun County and Georgia state officials had not anticipated was the influx of tourism in the wake of the production; several businesses, including riverboat tour companies, quickly set up shop to accommodate curious film tourists. Governor Carter sprang into action, setting up a state level Motion Picture and Television Advisory Committee that would be responsible for marketing Georgia as a production location as well as assisting productions in progress (Kaminsky, 1972). In advance of a promotional visit by Georgia state delegates to Hollywood in 1972, a half-page ad appeared in the *Hollywood Reporter* that included a picture of Jimmy Carter with a bold caption underneath reading: "Meet Jimmy Carter. The man who blew up a car, burned down a house, and changed the course of a river. All on cue." The ad copy described how the governor himself would be in Los Angeles for two days to discuss film production with any interested parties, prompting the slogan, "Georgia. We'll do anything to be in show business."

From Hollywood labor's perspective, Georgia was but one of many states vying for "runaway" dollars. In July 1974, *The Hollywood Reporter* declared Arizona the "domestic runaway capitol of the United States," contributing to an estimated $16 million in annual production revenues leaving the state of California (Tusher, 1974, p. 1). A string of major motion pictures, mostly Westerns, had been shot in Arizona in the previous year, including *The Trial of Billy Jack* (1974), *The Hanged Man* (1974), *Death Wish* (1974), and *Alice Doesn't Live Here Anymore* (1974). In fact, the state had become such a hot location commodity that some speculated it was the busiest production center in the United States, only surpassed by California and New York. Representatives from Arizona's State Film Commission and Office of Economic Planning and Development attributed the production boom to several factors, including unique locations such as the Grand Canyon and Superstition Mountains, good weather, and a concerted effort by state officials to ease the location permit process, known to be quite cumbersome in Los Angeles.

In 1984, Texas surpassed Arizona to become the third-busiest production location in the United States, with state film representatives touting a new $35 million state-of-the-art soundstage at the Dallas Communication Complex (Hulbert, 1984). The investment was far from foolhardy, as projects flocking to Texas at the time included high-profile, Oscar-winning and nominated films such as *Tender Mercies* (1983), *Terms of Endearment* (1983), *Silkwood* (1983), and *Places in the Heart* (1984). Hollywood producers working in Texas argued that it was the authenticity of locations there, and not the bottom line, driving the production surge (p. H11). Producers also commented on the "eagerness" of Texas crews and "starstruck property owners" compared to Hollywood, where workers were jaded and city residents were hostile, demanding exhorbitant location fees to film their properties. The Hollywood unions, however, argued that Texas was a haven of anti-unionism. Not only was the state out of the jurisdiction of the Screen Extras Guild, it also was a right-to-work state, where production crews could be comprised of both union and non-union workers without penalty. All totalled, productions in Texas were estimated to cost from 15 to 30 percent less than California, mostly due to labor savings.

By 1985, nearly every state in the United States had established a film office, with a concentration of competition coming from states all along the Atlantic coast: from New York and Massachussetts in the North, to the Carolinas and Florida in the South. Though a relative newcomer to film production, Massachussetts had an established television industry, with the venerable WGBH Boston providing the state with a national reputation for high quality public broadcasting and documentary production. But commercial hits like *Cheers* and *St. Elsewhere* had brought both positive attention and a 24 percent increase in tourism to the state, generating enthusiastic support from Governor Michael Dukakis for efforts to expand the industry in Massachussetts (Harmetz, 1985, p. C15). Dukakis expressed some sympathy for Los Angeles film workers hostile toward outside interests coming to their city to promote runaway production. While the governor declared his sensitivity "to the idea of going raiding" in Los Angeles, he also made clear that he'd do what he had to do to attract production to his state, even if it meant a trip to Hollywood to close a deal (Luther, 1984, p. OC1).

North Carolina, on the other hand, had caught the eye of powerhouse producer Dino De Laurentiis, who decided to build a production complex in the coastal town of Wilmington. His North Carolina Film Corporation was comprised of both sound stages and permanent outdoor sets, including urban streetscapes constructed for the film *The Year of the Dragon* (1985) that served as a stand-in for New York's Chinatown. For De Laurentiis, the North Carolina enterprise was purely a matter of economics: he could hire extras for

$35 a day, rather than the $91 a day charged for union extras in Hollywood. De Laurentiis also estimated that the street sets for *Dragon* would have cost roughly three times as much to build in Hollywood as compared to North Carolina due to the differential in union scales between the two locations. A little further down the coastline, Florida had also become a considerable concern for Hollywood unions with the opening of the Walt Disney World Theme Park in 1971. The California film community strongly disapproved of one of Hollywood's most venerable studios making such a major investment outside the state. In 1989, Disney became even more entrenched in Orlando with the construction of the Disney/MGM Studios—a combination resort, theme park, and working television and film production complex. Disney CEO Michael Eisner presided over the opening of the new park area, presenting a dedication plaque that immortalized the company's shifting understanding of Hollywood:

> The world you have entered was created by the Walt Disney Company and is dedicated to Hollywood—not a place on a map, but a state of mind that exists wherever people dream and wonder and imagine, a place where illusion and reality are fused by technological magic. We welcome you to a Hollywood that never was—and always will be. (Vagnini, 2009)

While Hollywood labor may have felt like Disney had abandoned them, it was clear that Disney felt in no way beholden to Hollywood as a situated place. It is also clear that Disney knew its audience and their expectations: they weren't necessarily looking for "authentic" experiences of place, either in film or in their visits to amusement parks. Rather, they could be satisfied with a fusion of "illusion and reality." Orlando was just as good a place as anywhere else to reconstruct some version of Hollywood—and perhaps one better than the original, "a Hollywood that never was," including a Hollywood without union problems. Florida was a right-to-work state, where unions could not impose sole jurisdiction over media production practices

In a year-end edition of the *Hollywood Reporter*, an article titled "Runaway Production: Home is Where the Shot is" considered the "war between the states" over production work (Newman, 1989). Ted Kaye, vice president of film and video production for Disney/MGM in Orlando, commented that the studio was indeed gunning for the number two spot behind Hollywood in terms of production business in the United States. With production budgets estimated at 20 percent under L.A. and New York's going rates, a growing community of production professionals, and few—if any—location permit requirements, Kaye felt it was only a matter of time before Orlando would live up to its nickname of "Hollywood East" (p. 84).

In response to the onslaught of domestic competition in the 1970s and 1980s, a call to arms went out among Hollywood's anti-runaway production labor interests. Only unlike previous decades, Hollywood labor managed to garner serious interest among California state legislators. Their activities included a series of public hearings on runaway production, a restructuring of the location permit system in Los Angeles, and the creation of a state film commission to promote and nurture the California industry. Los Angeles's location permit system was the first target for reform chosen by Hollywood's anti-runaway production contingency. Some labor representatives and public officials feared that the tangle of permits required to shoot in Los Angeles, and the time and energy spent running from one municipal agency to another to get them, was discouraging production work in Southern California. For instance, a film project that wanted to use locations in Santa Monica or Malibu was required to secure permits from Los Angeles County, the city of Santa Monica, the state of California, as well as permissions from local fire, police, and health offices (Funke, 1974, p. 135). The solution was the creation of the Los Angeles City One-Stop Film Coordination Office, where production and location managers could go to obtain all the necessary permits. In a 1975 interview with the *Hollywood Reporter*, L.A. Councilman Joel Wachs praised the newly established One-Stop office, attributing its inception with a reversal in runaway production and providing "a new spirit to both the industry and the community" (Wachs, 1975, p. 12). The following year, the *Los Angeles Times* showcased the success of the One-Stop office in a feature story about the "resurgence of street location shooting" in the city (Jones, 1976, p. C1). Coordinators from the newly re-titled City Inter-Departmental Committee for Economic Development (CICED) explained how one $50 permit issued by their office now replaced the roughly twenty different approvals needed to shoot in Los Angeles. They were also assisting with coordinating traffic and crowd control around congested city street locations, making movies like *Car Wash* (1976)—filmed almost entirely at the intersection of 6th and Rampart Boulevard—possible. CICED coordinator Bill Johnson bragged that in recent months he had facilitated as many as ten productions in progress in a six-block radius, which he believed was a sure sign that runaway productions were coming back to Los Angeles.

Around the same time that Los Angeles's one-stop permit office became operational, efforts were also being made to establish an industry coordinating office at the state level. As early as 1971, L.A. city officials, most notably Mayor Sam Yorty, had called for the establishment of a central coordinating agency that would "'more aggressively' halt 'runaway production,' particularly to nearby states" (Metropolitan, 1971, p. A2). The State Assembly responded in September 1974 with the creation of the Unit for Motion Picture Development. The official functions of the Unit included the implementation of promotional campaigns touting film locations around the state, assisting production companies with securing location permits, and facilitaing and coordinating efforts between local, state, and federal governments, and private sector groups in the service of motion picture productions (Motion Picture Development Unit, 1974). But within a year, the fate of the Motion Picture Unit was uncertain. Governor Edmund Brown, Jr. began dismantling the state's Department of Commerce, having concluded that issues of business development and international trade were better left to the private sector, including the motion picture industry.

In May 1975, however, California State Senator George Moscone attempted to salvage state services for the film industry by proposing the creation of a Department of Tourism and Motion Picture Production Development within the Business and Transportation Agency (California Senate Bill 1189, 1975). The new Motion Picture council was to be comprised of eleven representatives from the state legislature, local government, motion picture companies, and motion picture labor groups and professional organizations, to be appointed by the governor. Moscone and other proponents of the bill argued that the goals of the office of tourism and of the motion picture industry were essentially the same: to increase travel to and within California. And yet, the bill was opposed by key legislative groups, including the Business and Transportation Agency where the new department was to be located. These legislators saw SB 1189 as an attempt to resurrect the Department of Commerce, and with it the state's involvement in business and trade development: as stated in a handwritten note at the bottom of the Agriculture and Service committee's veto request, "The Phoenix rises from the ashes. A rose by any other name is still the Dept. of Commerce." Governor Brown eventually vetoed SB 1189, arguing that "[t]here is no credible evidence that a special state bureaucracy in California can promote tourism more effectively than the Chamber of Commerce and local business" (Brown Jr., 1975). It was also believed that California didn't need to make the kind of massive investment in promoting its film industry as other states were making for the simple fact that California had a global reputation as the home of the film industry.

One year later, efforts were renewed to not only revive but *expand* California's Motion Picture Development Unit. The biggest problem facing its proponents was funding: the Unit had received some modest funding from the Governor's Office and the legislative general fund, but under the condition that the program would be fiscally self-sufficient within the year. One plan to generate funds was introduced by State Senator Alan Robbins in April 1976, who proposed that the Motion Picture Development Council collect fees for the use of state owned property by motion picture productions (California Senate Bill 1620, 1976). A nearly identical bill was introduced to the State Assemby by Herschel Rosenthal in August (California Assembly Bill 3114,

1976), which was eventually signed into law by Governor Brown in September 1976. In addition to providing the Motion Picture Development Council with the means to sustain itself through service fees, the new statute allocated $50,000 in start-up funds for the implementation of the new service plan. With legislative legitimacy established and a funding structure in place, the Motion Picture Development Council (and its future forms) would become central to several anti-runaway production initiatives over the next several years.

The issue of runaway film production continued to grow in importance and visibility within the California legislature in the 1980s. The California Motion Picture, Television, and Commerical Industries Act of 1984 (California State Senate, 1984), sponsored by Senator Herschel Rosenthal, was considered the state's first offical anti-runaway legislation. The statute was created to fulfill "a need for concerted efforts by California state and local governments to provide an environment supportive of, and conducive to, the undertakings of the motion picture industry in this state" (p. 5910). Among its provisions were increased financial support for the Motion Picture Council, establishment of discounted permit fees for use of state property and employees for film production, and authorization of the Film Council and the California Film Office to coordinate statewide efforts in issuing various permits for film and television productions. Within a year, the Industries Act seemed to pay off, with a record number of film permits issued in Los Angeles (Gladstone, 1985). Much credit was given to Lisa Rawlins, the California Film Office's director, who described her job as "to stand at the border with with arms outstretched and say to film makers, 'Don't go away!'" (Harmetz, 1985, p. C15). Rawlins was allocated a $380,000 budget to promote production in California and to continue to simplify the state's notoriously prohibitive locations permit system. The state film office was also put in charge of assisting the development of local film commissions in over sixty communties throughout the state (Assembly Committee on Economic Development and New Technologies, 1985).

The California Motion Picture, Television, and Commerical Industries Act of 1984 also spurred a series of in-depth hearings around the state on the issue of runaway production. One of the most well-documented of these hearings was held in Monterey's City Hall on December 9, 1985 and served as a joint hearing of the State Assembly Committee on Economic Development and Technology (headed by Assemblyman Sam Farr), and the State Assembly Subcommittee on Sports and Entertainment (chaired by Assemblyman Gary Condit). The location of the hearings outside Los Angeles served a very specific purpose: the focus of the hearings was to be on the preservation of California's—and not just Hollywood's—film and television production industry. According to a report generated by the California Film Office and distributed at the hearings, out-of-state runaway production was responsible for an estimated $1 billion in production revenue losses in California in 1984; and of 156 films shot in the United States that year, 56 were shot entirely in California, 20 were shot partially in California, and 80 were shot entirely in other states. New York, Arizona, Texas, and Florida were named the top four "runaway" states (Assembly Committee on Economic Development and New Technologies, 1985, dsa1, p. 2).

Leaders from all sectors of the film industry were called to testify on runaway production, including producers, state officials, location managers, union representatives, and commissioners from municipal film offices around the state. The hearings began with testimony from Clint Eastwood—a Hollywood actor, producer, and director, and also a California native. Eastwood provided a practical yet sympathetic perspective on the domestic runaway production trend. He acknowledged that production costs were sometimes a motivation for shooting in other states—as an example, he described having rented a parking lot for three weeks in New Orleans at the same price he'd paid to rent parking in Los Angeles for one night. Eastwood also admitted that it was refreshing to work in communities where the residents were happy to have them there, whereas L.A. residents, who are frequently inconvenienced by film productions, could be quite hostile. Despite these shortcomings, Eastwood made it clear that he was still committed to supporting production in California, and the "comfort of being near home" (p. 8).

Lisa Rawlins of the California Film Office testified next, and immediately tried to reframe the critique levelled by Eastwood and other runaway producers that Los Angeleans had become too jaded with the production industry. She pointed out that the industry was important to many communities across the state, and not just Los Angeles—communities that were in dire need of the "economic shot in the arm" the film industry could provide and that would surely give productions a warm reception. And in an effort to open producers' eyes to locations around the state, Rawlins office was helping to organize a California locations trade show as well as weekend tours around the state for industry locations managers. Later in the interview, Assemblyman Condit asked Lisa Rawlins to comment directly on the legitimacy of the issue of runaway production: "I don't think that it is crippling the industry, and I don't think that it is necessarily crippling the state. But I think we're losing enough jobs and enough money to warrant our attention" (dsb2, p. 19). Rawlins was careul not to overstate the importance of domestic runaway film production to the problems faced by California's industry. At the same time, it seems evident that Rawlins was on a mission to deterritorialize the film industry from its problematic identity as strictly a Los Angeles industry. Even if it meant putting various California communities in direct competition with each other, the bottom line would be revenues generated for the state; and as the state film commissioner, that was her top priority.

Concerns over the potential loss of post-production work in Los Angeles, a key sector of the industry that thus far had remained relatively untouched by runaway production practices, were also addressed during the hearings. Jim McCabe, a locations manager for Universal Pictures, explained that, in fact, some elements of postproduction were increasingly being done on-location and outside Hollywood. In a discussion with Assemblyman Farr, McCabe explained how television shows like *Miami Vice* and *Magnum, P.I.*, shot in Florida and Hawaii respectively, were able to edit their shows on location. In short, these productions could fly an editor to their location, edit raw footage on-site, then transmit the final cut back to Hollywood via a satellite link. McCabe saw limitations to the use of technology for outsourcing post-production work, particularly visual and sound effects that required complex and expensive equipment only found in Los Angeles. All the same, his testimony on the role of technology in domestic runaway practices seemed to come as a revelation to Assemblyman Farr:

> *ASSEMBLYMAN FARR:* I'm hearing you say something I've never heard anybody say before, and that is another concern for runaway production, as technology improves, is that technology can run away from California as well.
>
> *MR. MC CABE:* Easily. (dsa3, pp. 13–14)

McCabe's testimony ended on the same question posed to state film commissioner Lisa Rawlins on the legitimacy of the issue of runaway film production. Perhaps in an act of self-preservation, McCabe hestitated to put the blame for production outsourcing on runaway producers, but instead shifted the focus to differences in localized production conditions: "I don't know if it's necessarily physically, producers getting on planes, and taking the raw stock, and going out of state to film it. Again, it's attitudinal. Runaway production in the sense that people are unhappy when they can't do the kind of work they'd like to do in their own state" (dsb4, pp. 2–3). It's interesting to note that McCabe reframed the runaway production issue not as a problem of foreign outsourcing, but as a matter of local and regional competition. McCabe also effectively avoided the issue of cost savings from one location to another. Rather, it is implicit in his comment about runaway production as a matter of attitude—if Hollywood could get an "attitude adjustment" and make conditions more amenable to producers and locations managers—then perhaps productions wouldn't have to leave the city or state.

Experts and academics from outside the film industry were also invited by the Assembly Committee on Economic Development and New Technologies to share their perspectives on runaway production. Susan Christopherson, whose work on film labor and regionalization have been cited throughout this book, was a visiting professor at UCLA at the time of the hearings and head of a special project funded by the Haines Foundation of Los Angeles that had analyzed changes occuring in the economic organization of the film industry. Christopherson seemed dubious toward the issue of runaway production, describing it as "an old idea" that had been around since the 1950s. By contrast, the UCLA project had been intended to deemphasize "attitudes and impressions, and anecdotal information" and shed light on the actual "locational patterns" occuring within the industry (dsb4, p. 4). Christopherson described 1973 as a watershed year, during which the industry experienced a shift from outsourcing production work to Europe—what the professor called "real runaway production"—to a trend in productions being staged all around the United States, and not just California. Despite the startling finding that 50 to 70 percent of U.S. motion picture production was being conducted outside Southern California, it was also found that Los Angeles' film labor force still accounted for 74 percent of all U.S. film labor, and was on the rise. Christopherson attributed this discrepancy between production volume and employment volume in Hollywood to the industry's transition from studio-based production to contractual or "per job" production hiring. So instead of having a small labor force working steady, forty-hour work weeks as had been the norm in the studio system, the newly emerging Hollywood industry had a large workforce working less frequently and for shorter stretches of time—an industry system that Christopherson believed pumped up the unemployment numbers and obscured the actual, subtantial amount of production work being done in Los Angeles.

Assemblymen Statham and Condit expressed concern over the fact that the UCLA report appeared to "deemphasize" and even "ignore" the issue of runaway production. Professor Christopherson responded that it was simply a matter of how one defined the film industry. For the purposes of the UCLA report, they had considered all stages of production as part of the industry: from equipment and prop rental companies to advanced technology services such as editing and special effects. Christopherson followed up by arguing that the term "runaway production" was too narrowly focused on the filming stage of production and therefore misrepresented the economic and employment landscape of the industry (dsb4, p. 12). The project's recommendation to legislators and state film interests was to nurture sectors of the industry still dominated by California, namely technology-oriented production services, financial backing, and creative development and "think tank" services.

The final group to testify at the hearings was comprised of film commissioners from various northern California communities. Joe O'Kane, director of San Jose's Film and Video Commission, spoke at length about the improvements being made by the California Film Office in coordinating and streamlining the state's industry. But while O'Kane agreed that the state had a problem with runaway production going to other states, he also observed that productions and communities almost wholly independent from Los Angeles were also developing across the country. Refering to the making of *Blood Simple* (1984) by Minneapolis natives Joel and Ethan Coen, "That was Minneapolis money, it was filmed in Texas, and posted in New York. It had nothing to do with California. The distribution came out of California, but everything else involving that production. . . . Filmmaking is becoming more regionalized" (Assemby Committee on Economic Development and Technology, 1985, December 9).

In the years following the Monterey hearings, the state legislature threw its support behind the California Film Commission and its mission to curb runaway production, introducing several bills to gaurantee the commission's operational budget, expand its staff, and fund its initiatives, such as the "one stop" location permit office (California Assembly Bill 3312, 1986; California Assembly Bill 3066, 1986; California Assembly Bill 3555, 1986; California Assembly Bill 2589, 1986; California Assembly Bill 7, 1987). In 1989, the Film Commission published a report on the "Economic Impact of the Film Industry in California," co-sponsored by the California Chamber of Commerce. Using industry statistics from 1987, the report found that California captured 70 percent of all U.S. feature film production and 87.5 percent of U.S. television production; everything above and beyond those figures was considered "runaway production" to other states (Economic Impact Study, 1989). Of particular note was the report's comparative data, looking at average production expenses in key competitive production communities across the country, including Dallas, Miami, Chicago, and New York. Only one non-U.S. location was included in the production expense comparisons—Vancouver. Though Vancouver was found to have the most cost saving potential for runaway producers, mostly due to exchange rate (CDN$1.25 to US$1 at the time) and lower hourly rates for crew, the report seemed to dismiss Vancouver as an immediate threat, pointing out that crews there were still generally inexperienced.

Of more concern to Hollywood production workers was the increasing number of runaway productions making their way across the border to Mexico, a mere 135 miles away from Los Angeles. In fact, Mexico was closer than many of the states that had caused jurisdictional consternation for the Hollywood unions, including Florida and North Carolina, which perhaps explains why runaway productions in Mexico were frequently framed within discussion of stateside runaway production. The Hollywood production community argued that due to the shared topography of Southern California and much of Northern Mexico, there was no need to take productions to Mexico—anything meant to look like Mexico could certainly be recreated and shot in and around Los Angeles with union crews. Sam Peckinpah, one of the most successful Hollywood filmmakers in the 1970s and 1980s, was particularly active in Mexico and particularly antagonistic toward Hollywood union gripes about runaway production. Tensions between the director and the unions were rooted in his consistent choice to film outside Hollywood: *The Ballad of Cable Hogue* (1970) in New Mexico, Arizona, and Nevada; *Straw Dogs* (1971) in England; and *The Getaway* (1972) in Texas. In 1969, Peckinpah filmed one of his most successful films, *The Wild Bunch*, in Durango and Cuahíla, Mexico.

Upon his return to Mexico in 1973 to film *Bring Me the Head of Alfredo Garcia*, the Hollywood unions launched an attack against Peckinpah, calling him out on what they saw as runaway film practices. In October 1973, several film unions banded together at a conference in Detroit, calling themselves the National Conference of Motion Picture and Television Unions (NACOMPTU). Member unions included IATSE, AFTRA, SAG, and NABET. Their first order of business was to adopt a resolution condemning Peckinpah as an unabashed runaway director. The unions had been particularly riled when Peckinpah had declared in *Variety*, "For me Hollywood no longer exists. I have decided to stay in Mexico because I believe I can make my pictures with greater freedom here" (Kirk, 1973, p. 1). NACOMPTU called for a boycott of Peckinpah's films by its members, and picketing of theaters where they were being shown. The *Los Angeles Times* interviewed Peckinpah on location in Mexico, seeking a response to the unions' threatened boycott. A rather unflattering portrait of the director and his producer, Martin Baum, was conveyed in the article:

> Sam Peckinpah chomped, almost defiantly, on a shank of goat in a Mexican cantina, picked up a tortilla with his free hand and denounced a threatened boycott of his work.
>
> Producer Martin Baum laughed and stabbed a finger at the goat and tortillas. "You can't get that in Los Angeles," he said. "Tell that to the unions." (Meisler, 1973, p. F26)

Peckinpah defended his choice to film in Mexico based on location authenticity: the story of *Bring Me the Head of Alfredo Garcia* was set in contemporary Mexico. Peckinpah also argued that he was misquoted by *Variety*, having said he would never work for Metro-Goldwyn-Mayer and not that he would never work in Hollywood again; the director was locked in a dispute with the studio over "unauthorized" editing of his film *Pat Garrett and Billy the Kid* (1973). With these clarifications, Martin Baum dismissed the unions' accusations that their current film was a runaway production: "I think that the unions have a good case with the wrong picture. I think they picked on Sam because he is a colorful man. It guarantees their getting into the papers. There's been more written on this picture than on Watergate" (p. F27). The unions' beef with Peckinpah would eventually blow over. But anxieties over film labor outsourcing to Canada and Mexico would only be exacerbated in the following decades, particularly in the wake of the North American Free Trade Agreement of 1994.

The development of the discourse on domestic runaway film production in the 1970s and 1980s coincided with an evolving regionalization of the film industry, both in terms of its political economy and cultural identity. Far from being a subtle development, many in the industry recognized and commented on the new regional nature of industry competition during this time. But what is also apparent is that few in the industry saw the regionalization of film production as part of the larger, globalizing trend in Hollywood film production that had already been set in motion in previous decades. The final evidence can be seen in the grouping of non-U.S. production communities such as Vancouver with domestic runaway locations in the Calfornia Film Commission's 1989 report. Though national exchange rates were a factor, the competition for runaway production work was not framed as one between the United States and Canada, but between Vancouver and Hollywood, or California more generally. In this way, the discourse of domestic runaway production demonstrated that the development of the new division of cultural labor was (and continues to be) dependent upon the coordination of economic policies across governments. But contrary to Miller, et al.'s (2001) thesis, the coordination of economic policies friendly to multinational corporations was neither limited to the level of the nation-state nor to international trade and production policies. Instead, as predicted by Pietrse (2004), we see a complex negotiation between municipal interests (e.g., L.A.'s one-stop permit office), state agencies (e.g., the California Film Commission and the state legislature), as well as national and international policy makers (e.g., federally-mandated tax incentives and labor policies in Canada and Mexico).

That said, Miller et al. (2001) accurately describe the role of technology in the New International Division of Cultural Labor as a tool in securing "capital's continuing domination of labor" rather than as a tool for labor's liberation. Regardless of the fact that productions were only "running" to other states and cities within the U.S., technology was used to further immobilize Hollywood labor; or as Massey (1984) might describe it, the use of technology increased the power of above-the-line labor by giving them more control over the "time-space compression" of the production process—shifting production work like editing quickly from one place to another via satellite technology—while at the same time weakening below-the-line labor by emphasizing their "differential mobility" (p. 150). The same process was occuring in the outsourcing of animation work, but on an international scale, once again demonstrating the interconnection between local, regional, and international production processes in globalization, as well as the crucial role of technology in managing this complex, multi-levelled division of labor.

CONCLUSION

Two major shifts in the organization and management of the film and television industries in the 1970s and 1980s are argued to have played a major role in shaping the debates over runaway production during this time: the localizing and regionalizing of competition for production labor, and the integration of technology for the management of film and television production.

In their battles against runaway animation in the 1970s and 1980s, Hollywood animators recognized that the studios were attempting to segment the production process in the same way reflected in the media capital model, with animation storyboarding and design allotted to the more skilled Hollywood labor, and the less skilled and labor intensive ink and paint work outsourced to inexpensive non-union labor abroad. Labor was able to briefly reintegrate and reterritorialize the process through the negotiation of their "runaway clause." But through the de-skilling and technologizing of portions of the animation process, a key strategy used by transnational media industries to mobilize and outsource production services (Schiller, 2000; Mosco, 2006), the animators eventually lost their "runaway wars" with the Hollywood animation studios.

Discussions of runaway television production and domestic runaway production brought attention to the overlapping of local, regional, national, and international production interests for emerging transnational media industries (Morley & Robins, 1995). Though television had been experienced mostly as a localized medium—reflecting community, regional, and national values—the rise of cable and global distribution systems such as satellite highlighted the increasingly transnational nature of the industry and the production of its content. The story of runaway television production provides some insight into labor's struggle to re-territorialize television production as a local and regional process as transnational media interests sought to de-territorialize it and expand the distribution of television content to global markets. Similarly, debates over domestic runaway production seem to reflect the integration of local and regional production labor forces into the highly competitive New International Division of Cultural Labor (NICL) (Miller, et al., 2001). This takes on a disorienting effect within the discourse, with competition for Hollywood production work represented in all manner of local and regional threats: on one day it was Arizona, the next, Orlando, and on yet another, Mexico, etc. Christopherson (2005) has argued that the regionalization of media industry competition since the 1970s was meant to create just this kind of disorientation among union production labor—with local and regional labor forces more concerned with identifying and undercutting the competition (oftentimes other Locals belonging to the same union) than joining forces with them to create more equitable labor conditions. Put in another way, the regionalization of labor competition and the resulting discourse of domestic runaway production have served (and continue to serve) the hegemonic needs of transnational media industries, who ultimately benefit from labor infighting.

NOTES

1. Drawing of intermediate animation frames between the dominant action frames.
2. Just as the *Wizard of Oz* (1939) used "Somewhere over the Rainbow" as a metaphor for the transition to color film, Disney included a digitally inked and painted rainbow in the final scene of *The Little Mermaid* (1989) to mark their first major foray into digital animation (Kerlow, 2004).
3. According to IATSE Local 839, Disney's animation staff rapidly expanded after 1985: from 125 to 1,500 in 1995. Similarly, Local 839's membership has swollen to 3,000 in recent years (IATSE Local 839, 2000).

Chapter Four

The Canadian Film Industry and "So-Called" Runaway Production[1]

A notable upsurge in interest in runaway film production occurred in the 1990s and early 2000s: trade press coverage skyrocketed, with *Variety* and *The Hollywood Reporter* together publishing over 1,200 news items on runaway production between 1990 and 2010—more than all previous decades combined. Greater volume in popular and trade press coverage has been accompanied by an increase in academic research on runaway production. Greg Elmer and Mike Gasher (2005) compiled an excellent edited collection outlining several issues relevant to contemporary runaway production, including global media market development, the outsourcing of digital post-production work, and the construction of place and audiences through runaway films. Toby Miller, et al. (2001), Thomas Guback (1969), Manjunath Pendakur (1990), and Janet Wasko (2003), among others, have addressed runaway production within their various studies of the political economy of global Hollywood. One theme that emerges across this group of popular, trade, and academic press coverage of runaway production is an intense focus on Canada as a runaway location.

In this chapter, I pick up the thread of Canadian runaway production, highlighting some of the key developments in this discursive shift, including debates over Canadian industry subsidies. But given the prolific coverage of the Canadian situation from a U.S. industry perspective, the majority of this chapter will be spent examining an aspect of the discourse that has been largely ignored—the construction of a counter-discourse to "so-called" runaway production by the Canadian film industry. Central within the Canadian counter-discourse is a justification for industry subsidies and Canadian-Hollywood co-productions as last lines of defense against runaway U.S. cultural imperialism. The Canadian runaway film industry is also argued to be a part of a new, globalized film industry, in which even the most unlikely places—Canada, New Zealand, Romania—may become competitive forces, perhaps to the point of emancipating themselves from their overly-dependent service relationship with Hollywood. But as will be discussed in the final section of this chapter, the elevation of Canada's status within the global film industry in the 1990s and 2000s has been tempered with a sense of paranoia over reverse runaway production—productions running to other foreign locations, between Canadian provinces, and even back to the United States.

As anticipated in discussions of Canadian runaway production in the previous chapter, the interactive debates between Hollywood and Canadian film interests is argued to reflect the industry's shift toward a multi-directional system of "media capitals." As explained by Curtin (2003), the current global film industry is no longer one that strictly turns on the axis of Hollywood, but is rather an industry with several large nodes that both compete and collaborate within the New International Division of Cultural Labor (Miller, Govil, McMurria & Maxwell, 2001). It will also be argued that Canadian and U.S. constructions of runaway film production represent a continuation of the regionalization of film labor noted in relation to domestic runaway production in the 1970s and 1980s; a trend in which localized labor communities, often represented by the same unions, are isolated and forced into competition by the multinational corporations who control the global film industry (Christopherson, 2005).

Finally, the Canadian discourse of "so-called" runaway production, and specifically debates over national and provincial subsidies for their industry, are argued to function within a larger meaning system of "governmentality"—in which culture is conceived as "an instrument of government . . . to be applied in the service of government" (Bennett, 1992, p. 25). Thinking through the concept of governmentality, the contention is made that the Canadian government has effectively used its film industry as a means for liberalizing and commodifying "Canadian-ness" in exchange for a more powerful position within the NICL. And to a large degree, the Canadian public has willingly accepted the dilution of their Canadian-ness in exchange for an identity more closely linked to the glamour, and fortunes, of Hollywood. But this political and economic rendering of Canadian-ness is in large part a co-construction with the Hollywood film industry—a finely tuned "cultural technology," deftly capable at sanitizing and commodifying cultural products for the global media market.

SETTING THE STAGE FOR CANADIAN RUNAWAY PRODUCTION

In the 1980s, Canada was still barely a blip on the radar of Hollywood's anti-runaway production lobbyists, with Canada warranting only a handful of mentions in the popular and trade press during that time (e.g., Gendel, 1986). Even when Canada turned up in discussions of runaway production in the 1980s, Hollywood labor tended to dismiss the Canadian threat: in their opinion, the amateurish runaway movies-of-the-week and low-budget TV series coming out of Vancouver and Toronto dispelled any concerns over Canada's runaway potential. But these Hollywood castoff projects began to add up by the late 1980s, with some sources estimating Hollywood runaway investments in Canadian productions at around $400 million (Bates, J., 1987). Real money was suddenly at stake, and from this point forward, Canada increasingly became the focal point of social, political, and economic discussions of runaway film production in the United States.

The debate over the impact of Canadian runaway production on U.S. film labor has been primarily constructed around economy: specifically, that the primary motivation for Hollywood producers to run to Canada has been to save money over comparable production costs in Los Angeles and other U.S. locations. And when Hollywood producers have argued that they needed to go to Canada in search of location authenticity (aka creative runaways), U.S. labor groups have countered that very few Canadian runaway projects have featured story lines set in Canada. In reality, Hollywood producers could get more for their money in Canada due to the strength of the U.S. dollar in the 1990s and early 2000s. In 1990, US$1 exchanged for CDN$1.17. By 1998, the U.S. dollar traded for CDN$1.48, finally peaking in 2002 at CDN$1.57. On this factor alone, a producer could anticipate increasing the value of their production budget by more than 30 percent simply by taking their project to Canada over shooting in the United States, an extraordinary value when considering projects running into the tens of millions of U.S. dollars—many topping US$100 million in the 2000s. An example would be *X2: X-Men United* (2003), filmed primarily in Ontario and British Columbia for a reported budget of US $110 million (Mendelson, 2016).

Along with an attractive exchange rate, Hollywood runaway producers in the early 1990s also saw Canada as a haven from what they argued to be Los Angeles's costly production regime, including location permits and soundstage rental fees, costs for police and fire department presence, and union labor wages. This was particularly relevant for producers of low-budget television series and movies-of-the-week, clambering to supply programming to fill the needs of ever-expanding cable networks. Leading the early wave of Canadian runaway television production in the late 1980s and early 1990s was Hollywood producer Stephen J. Cannell. A native Los Angeleno, Cannell had produced and written a string of small screen hits including *The Rockford Files* (1974–1980), *The Greatest American Hero* (1981–1983), and *The A-Team* (1983–1987). Though Cannell was at the top of his game in the 1980s, he and his business partners complained bitterly of the lack of financial support for their hour-long episodic programs: network license fees that were meant to offset a substantial portion of production costs had stagnated at around $800,000 per hour-long episode in 1986, leaving producers to absorb upward of $500,000 in additional expenses per episode (Harris, 1986). The federal government had also retracted a 6⅔ percent Investment Tax Credit (ITC) around this time—a small but significant sum that Hollywood producers had relied on since the mid 1970s to take the edge off production costs. Under these increasingly difficult circumstances, Cannell Productions' chief operating officer, Michael Dubelko, justified their venture into low-cost Canadian production: it was saving their company roughly $250,000 a week (p. A1).

As luck would have it, Cannell Productions hit a homerun with their Canadian TV project *21 Jump Street*. Filmed in Vancouver, B.C. from 1987 to 1991, the series depicted the life of an undercover police officer—played by Johnny Depp—posing as a high school student in a large, unidentified U.S. city. Along with launching Depp's career, *21 Jump Street* also helped forge Vancouver's reputation as a viable option for high-quality Hollywood productions. Emboldened by success, Cannell expanded his Vancouver enterprise in 1989 to include North Shore Studios. With legitimate production facilities in place, other high-profile Hollywood projects followed, including *The X-Files* (1993–2002), *Catwoman* (2004), *The Fog* (2005), and *The Lizzie Maguire Movie* (2003). Though Cannell turned his attention to a career writing crime novels in the mid 1990s and had little direct involvement with North Shore Studios thereafter, the studio stands as a testament to his early investment in Vancouver's film production renaissance in the 1990s and 2000s, and is now recognized as Canada's largest production facility; an achievement revered within the Canadian film and television production community, and reviled by Hollywood production labor.

Runaway Hollywood film producers following in Cannell's footsteps in the 1990s found even more financial incentives waiting for them in Canada in the form of industry subsidies and tax credits. In two of the highest profile international trade negotiations involving the United States and Canada—the Free Trade Agreement (FTA) in 1988 and the North American Free Trade Agreement (NAFTA) in 1993—Canada successfully lobbied to exclude cultural industries from the final treaties (Hoskins, Finn, & McFadyen, 1996). Their argument was that U.S. media were overwhelming their market and stifling the growth of indigenous media industries: in 2004, U.S. imports were estimated to represent 75 percent of Canadian television programming and 95 percent of their movie viewership, generating around $1.3 billion in revenues for U.S. conglomerates from sales of theater tickets, DVDs, and other media goods to Canadian consumers (Hoskins, Finn, & McFadyen, 1996, p. 75; Neil Craig and Associates, 2004, p. 3).

The exclusion of cultural products from the free trade agreements with the United States gave the Canadian government the power to create various economic incentives, namely industry subsidies and tax credits, to encourage the development and distribution of commercially competitive and culturally unique Canadian media products. This policy move did not sit well with American media interests. However, Canadian Minister of Heritage Sheila Copps, part of the NAFTA negotiating team that secured the cultural exemption for Canada, defended the government's aggressive cultural policy agenda with the U.S.: "We are not a 51st State, and if we don't have a regulatory framework to keep Canadian television and to try to create a climate for Canadian film, we won't have culture and we won't have country" (Cuthbert, 1996, p. 1). As intimated by Copps, the Canadian film and television industries were the intended beneficiaries of culture industry protections resulting from the NAFTA, with substantial federal and provincial tax subsidies put in place shortly after the negotiations.

The Canadian Film or Video Production Tax Credit (CPTC) and the Film or Video Production Services Tax Credit (PSTC) were the two major subsidies created by the Department of Canadian Heritage. Established in 1995, the CPTC was intended to support indigenous productions, initially providing a 12 percent tax rebate for net production expenditures, and then upgraded in 2005 to a 25 percent tax credit for "the eligible labor costs of a Canadian-controlled production corporation which produces Canadian film or video productions" (Canadian Audio-Visual Certification Office, 2004, *CPTC*, pp. 4–5). Beneficiaries of the CPTC include *Corner Gas* (January 2004–April 2009), a popular television series produced by the Canadian Television Network depicting the life of a gas station attendant in the fictional town of Dog River, Saskatchewan.

While the stringent conditions of the CPTC seemed to comply with the objectives of the NAFTA cultural exemption—to protect and bolster indigenous Canadian film and television industries—the provisions of the Film or Television Service Tax Credit (PSTC) were more outwardly focused. Created a few years after the CPTC in 1997, the stated objective of the PSTC was to encourage the employment of Canadian citizens, regardless of the national affiliation of the production, or the "Canadianness" of the content. The PSTC originally provided an 11 percent credit for "qualifying Canadian labor expenditures" for film and television projects staged in Canada. The subsidy was increased to a 16 percent rebate in 2003 for productions with budgets of at least CDN$1,000,000 (approx. US$645,000 at the time) (Canadian Audio-Visual Certification Office, *PSTC*, 2004, p. 8). In the case of the PSTC, the qualifying definition of "Canadian" labor required only that the persons were residents of Canada when payments were made, and that all services were performed by said labor on Canadian soil.

Though the tax credit under the PSTC was less generous than the CPTC, it appeared to create the desired incentive for foreign productions when combined with exchange rate savings and provincial tax credits. In February 2010, locally produced projects in British Columbia could receive combined federal and provincial tax credits totaling an astounding 78.5 percent (B.C. Film Commission, 2010, February 28). Tax credits for foreign productions staged in B.C. were still quite generous, with the province offering a 33 percent credit in addition to the federal PSTC credit of 16 percent. Additional "regional" and "distant location" credits were also made available for productions using B.C. locations outside the more desirable Vancouver area, providing another 12 percent credit on top of the base provincial and federal credits, for a 61 percent tax incentive for those willing to go a little farther afield (B.C. Film Commission, 2010, February 28).

Most Hollywood-backed productions filmed in Canada have been made with the help of the PSTC subsidy, including Ang Lee's critically acclaimed *Brokeback Mountain* (2005). According to production interests on either side of the border, Ang Lee in fact wanted to shoot the film in Wyoming where the original short story was set (Dinoff, 2006, p. 28; McKay, 2006, p. E09). His initial dissatisfaction with the choice to shoot in Canada was expressed in an article about the film, featured on Wyoming's official tourism website: "One day I was shooting some [Canadian] mountain peaks and they asked me what to write in the script supervising notes. I said, 'a cheap imitation of Wyoming" (Shrimpton, 2006). But with a relatively modest budget of $14 million, the film's producers contended that shooting on location in Wyoming would have been economically impractical due to the lack of industry infrastructure in the state (e.g., labor, equipment rental companies, soundstages) to support a large film production (Dinoff, 2006). Tom Cox of Alberta Film Entertainment, one of the executive producers of the film, explained that in Alberta, where much of the film was shot, skilled labor and equipment could be brought in from nearby Vancouver (McKay, 2006). By partnering with the Alberta Film Entertainment (AFE) company, Lee and the U.S.-producing company Focus Features (an affiliate of NBC Universal) could claim no less than 35 percent in federal and provincial tax credits for labor expenditures (p. E09).

There's little doubt that Canada's federal and provincial production subsidies were, and continue to be, instrumental in the astronomical growth of their film and television industries. Toronto, Montreal, and Vancouver have emerged as globally competitive production centers—the latter ranked the third-largest in North America behind New York and Hollywood (British Columbia Film Commission, 2010, July; Sinoski, 2016, April 8). Though Hollywood runaway producers greatly benefited from Canada's subsidy system, below-the-line labor groups like the Film and Television Action Committee

(FTAC) contended that Canada's film subsidies were anti-competitive and specifically designed to lure away their jobs. But unlike previous decades, the complaints and accusations of Hollywood labor were met by equally vehement defenses and counter-accusations from Canadian labor interests who defiantly reconstructed Hollywood's outsourcing discourse as "so-called" runaway production in their own popular and trade press.

SO-CALLED RUNAWAY PRODUCTION: THE CANADIAN COUNTER-DISCOURSE

In the 1990s and 2000s, a highly contentious relationship developed between the U.S. and Canadian film communities over the issue of runaway film production. On the one hand, Hollywood labor saw Canadian industry subsidies as an abuse of their negotiated free trade cultural exemption, and called for U.S. sanctions against Canadian runaway productions benefitting from the subsidies. Canadian industry representatives, on the other hand, argued that "so-called" runaway production was merely a corrective for years of American media cultural imperialism in Canada. As in other instances of runaway production, the adversarial debates between U.S. and Canadian labor over runaway production are argued to reflect competing discourses of "deterritorialization" and "reterritorialization" (Canclini, 1995). For Canadian film workers, it was most beneficial to construct Canadian-U.S. film productions as part of a larger trend toward globalized film production, in which the industry abides by no territorial boundaries; for U.S. film workers, it was imperative to defend and redefine the territorial boundaries of the film industry around its historical base in Hollywood. What results are three primary counter-arguments made against so-called runaway film production by the Canadian film industry: a narrative of cultural imperialism, which constructed the so-called runaway production debate as hypocritical and inaccurate in light of the United States's historically privileged media trade relationship with Canada; a pro-globalization narrative, which described the rhetoric of runaway production as archaic and the production relationship between the United States and Canada as cooperative within a transnationalized film industry; and finally, an emancipation narrative that envisioned an internationally competitive and influential Canadian media industry freed from its reliance on U.S. runaway investment.

On one level, Canadian counter-discourses to runaway film production challenged Hollywood's hegemonic grip over the global film industry; production labor in Vancouver and Toronto presumed to compete with Hollywood and U.S. labor on a level playing field. However, Susan Christopherson

(2005) has argued that such instances of "labor localism" tend not to empower labor from one community or another, but rather support the "divide and conquer" strategies of multinational media conglomerates who benefit most from forcing regional and national labor into direct competition with each other. And in this sense, the discourse—and counter-discourse—of runaway film production is argued to *serve*, and not challenge, the hegemonic interests of MNC's by dividing Canadian and U.S. labor into competing camps, even though they are represented by many of the same unions and guilds.

On another level, it could be argued that the counter discourses to runaway film production represent an ongoing struggle by the Canadian production community to overcome what Appadurai (1996) has called transnational "production fetishism":

> . . . an illusion created by contemporary transnational production loci that masks translocal capital, transnational earnings flows, global management, and often faraway workers (engaged in various kinds of high-tech putting-out operations) in the idiom and spectacle of local (sometimes even worker) control, national productivity, and territorial sovereignty. (p. 42)

Through the discourse of so-called runaway film production, Canadian film interests desperately tried to construct the successes of their film and television industries as the result of a cooperative, if not independent, relationship with Hollywood studios and producers. Similarly, Canadian government officials repeatedly defended their industry subsidy system as primarily beneficial to Canadian—and not Hollywood—film industries. Instead, I argue that Canadian film centers like Vancouver were operating under an "illusion" of localism and "territorial sovereignty," when in fact they were just as vulnerable as Hollywood labor to the whims of multinational media corporations truly in charge of the New International Division of Cultural Labor (Miller, et al., 2001).

Runaway Cultural Imperialism

The first distinctive challenge to runaway film production identified in the Canadian press relied on the contentious thesis of cultural imperialism. It is a concept closely linked to theories of globalization, describing the dominant flow of cultural products, such as media programming, from one nation or culture into others, subordinating the latter's indigenous cultural production and consumption (Schiller, H.,1976; Schiller, H., 1969). While cultural imperialism is not a universally accepted construct (e.g., Appadurai, 1996; Bertrand, 1987, p. 270; Kraidy, 2005; Negus & Román-Velázquez, 2000), it appears to have formed a central logic in discussions of the media trade and production relationships between the United States and Canada in the Canadian press.

The stage for the cultural imperialism narrative was set by the U.S. release of the Monitor report on runaway production in 1999. The Monitor Report (1999), sponsored by the Screen Actors and Directors Guilds of America, explicitly quantified the damages done to the U.S. film industry by the migration of film production to non-U.S. locations. Several runaway destinations were discussed in the report, including Australia and the U.K. However, Canada was clearly framed as the primary offender, with 81 percent of U.S.-backed film productions made abroad in 1998 said to have gone to there—about 232 productions in 1998 compared to 63 in 1990 (p. 3). The report estimated the total loss of direct production expenditures for the U.S. film industry at US$2.8 billion, with U.S. job losses cited at 23,500 and counting (p. 16). A similar report was sponsored by Vice President Al Gore and released by the U.S. Department of Commerce in 2001, which corroborated the Monitor report's findings. It also focused much attention on Canada, putting the country at the top of its list of "principal foreign destinations of runaway film production" (p. 46).

Several Hollywood labor interests rallied around the findings of the runaway production reports, including the Film and Television Action Committee (FTAC). Formed in the spring of 1999, the FTAC was a film industry labor coalition, with key members from several Hollywood unions including the International Alliance of Theatrical and Stage Employees, the Screen Actors Guild, and the Teamsters (About the FTAC, 2007). The group's chairman was Jackson "Jack" DeGovia, president of the Hollywood IATSE's Art Directors Local 876 and a seasoned Hollywood production designer of over twenty-five years, with film credits including *Die Hard* (1988), *Sister Act* (1992), and *Speed* (1994). DeGovia, like his predecessor Roy Brewer, originally hailed from Oklahoma; also like Brewer, DeGovia seemed to embrace his role as a firebrand within Hollywood's anti-runaway production movement, engaging in several contentious battles with Canadian industry representatives in the following years.

In the wake of the Monitor Report release in the summer of 1999, DeGovia organized several large-scale rallies to admonish Canadian runaway production, while also showing support for proposed California film industry tax credit bills AB 358 and 484, authored by Assemblypersons Scott Wildman (D-Burbank) and Sheila Kuehl (D-Santa Monica), respectively. On July 6, 1,000 film workers from Los Angeles and Northern California, accompanied by a three-mile convoy of various production vehicles, gathered at the Capitol building in Sacramento for a noon rally; according to DeGovia, the vehicles were meant to represent the extraordinary production resources of California—camera cranes, grip trucks, dressing trailers—sitting idle due to the Canadian production exodus (Madigan, 1999, July). On August 15, around 5,000 film workers—the largest of the FTAC gatherings—marched along Hollywood Boulevard, chanting "Bring Hollywood Home" and wearing t-shirts depicting the Canadian maple leaf at the center of a bull's eye. Gathered in front of the Pantages Theatre in the heart of Hollywood, Jack DeGovia addressed the crowd, lamenting the impact of foreign subsidies on California's industry: "We are not a commodity. This rally is not the last. These bills are not the last. We will not stand by and let foreign governments buy our lives and our families" (Fritz, 1999). The FTAC had an uphill battle trying to convince California governor Gray Davis of the necessity of tax breaks for one of the state's most successful industries. But rather than flaming out on the governor's desk, Senate Bill 756 (a combined version of the original Assembly Bills 358 and 484) languished and "died on file" in the California Senate in November 2000.

As the FTAC and California legislators ramped up their efforts to stop runaway Canadian production in the late 1990s, Canadian journalists and film workers responded strongly to what they perceived to be the unfair demonization of the Canadian film industry. One Canadian reporter mocked such characterizations, suggesting U.S. anti-runaway activists might prefer the names "Darth Vancouver, and the evil Canadian movie-of-the-week empire" or "Vancouver—home to the cinematic maquiladores of the north" over "Hollywood North" (Burgess, 1999, p. C4). To completely invalidate the issue, the Canadian press generally referred to Hollywood's outsourcing complaints as "so-called runaway production" (e.g., Kelly, 2002, October; Powell, 2000).

The Canadian film industry also challenged the findings of the U.S. Monitor report, releasing their own report in 2004, prepared by Neil Craig Associates. As stated in its opening paragraphs, "People in the Canadian film industry feel that Canada continues to be attacked unfairly, based on the inflated claims made in the Monitor Report and recent scaremongering. . . . The results of this study dispel many of the myths perpetuated by [that report]" (Neil Craig and Associates, 2004, p. 2). The much-anticipated study painted a very different picture of the media trade relationship between the United States and Canada, including in its figures not only the revenues gained by Canada from U.S.-backed film productions (around US$1.17 billion for 1998), but also revenues paid back to the U.S. media industry in the form of cinema admissions, sales and rentals of videos and DVDs, and broadcast licenses. With revenues paid out for United States media goods and services estimated at US$1.3 billion, the Neil Craig report noted a continuing Canadian cultural trade deficit to the United States (p. 3), and therefore any discussion of the economic relationship between the U.S. and Canadian media industries had to include a complete picture of all related profits and losses—from production through consumption. Inspired by the Neil Craig report, the Canadian news media often mirrored the sentiment that Canadians were entitled to work on U.S.-financed film productions considering the mass consumption of U.S. media products. As Patrick Whitely of Film Ontario commented, "Look at the billions of dollars worth of American product that we consume in this country. I believe we have a right to be part of the manufacturing of that product" (Bracken, 2004, p. 1).

It was also argued that efforts by domestic media producers to gain an economic or cultural foothold in their own country were being stymied by U.S. media saturation in Canada. One filmmaker explained how even Canadian independent projects often came to rely financially on the U.S. media industry, both directly and indirectly: "Most B.C. filmmakers are now doing a couple of shows of their own and then they move into the service sector to work for the Americans. It's the only way they can survive financially" (Morgan, 2001, p. F2). A journalist from the Canadian film trade magazine *Playback* made a similar argument regarding the impact of co-production on the domestic industry, while also questioning the way so-called Canadian production revenues had been described by U.S. runaway reports. In their estimation, it was "a wash": $1.9 billion in American production investment in Canada was payback for the country's $1.5 billion contribution to American networks in the form of media distribution and consumption revenues (Vamos, 2004, p. 14).

Other commentators bemoaned Los Angeles's inevitable talent drain on the Canadian production community, luring away the country's best writers, directors, and actors, and further crippling the development of a viable domestic industry. In an article titled "Runaway Production in Reverse," Ontario-born actor David Hewlett, best known for his work on the *Stargate* television series, explained the dilemma: Even when Canadians could create successful domestic productions, their legitimacy as actors and filmmakers was inevitably dependent upon affiliations with Hollywood (Howell, 2001, p. 8). And what Hollywood had that Canada didn't was a historically and materially constructed system of institutions that functioned to reinforce its place at the center of the motion picture universe. For Canadian film laborers like Hewlett, it was evident that Canada's film industry was no match for the overwhelming historical and cultural legitimacy of Hollywood, and success in the global film industry required being situated at the geographic center, and not the periphery, of pop cultural meaning-making in Hollywood.

Finally, there were those who described the cultural subsidies offered by the Canadian government—subsidies meant to encourage indigenous media production, but more often diverted to U.S. productions in Canada through policy loopholes—as the country's only defense against the overwhelming presence of U.S. cultural imperialism. According to industry editorialist Susan Tolusso (2001), ". . . even that vague definition of Canadianness would evaporate" (p. 6) without the subsidies, making them worth whatever Hollywood service industry work they also incentivized.

Discussions of runaway film production and cultural imperialism in the Canadian press reflected what Negus & Román-Velázquez (2000) have identified as the "homogenization of culture" argument (p. 338), relying heavily on the notion that global audiences are vulnerable dupes, readily absorbing all U.S.-centric ideologies coded in media content to the exclusion of their own localized cultural knowledges and practices, and subsequently evolving into an Americanized global monoculture. Canadian culture, as both a framework of meaning-making for media audiences and a practice in the production of media, was depicted as rapidly dissolving under the tide of U.S. cultural influence. Even "so-called runaway production," described by many Canadian film workers as a long-overdue balancing of the media trade relationship that has long benefitted the United States, was ultimately constructed as an expression of U.S. cultural imperialism: American-developed and -financed productions could assume Canadian national identity for tax purposes with little or no responsibilities for representing Canadian culture on the screen. Even the descriptor "Canadian" had been colonized by U.S. media industries, throwing into question the real Canadian contribution to any productions identifying themselves as such.

Pro-Globalization

A second prominent theme identified within Canadian counterarguments to runaway film production was "pro-globalization." This theme was characterized by the construction of global industry as a positive force, "creating 'new markets,' breaking down barriers, and disrupting previous routines and a settled sense of distance between different people and places" (Negus & Román-Velázquez, 2000, p. 329). Pro-globalization discussions of runaway film production described a cooperative and harmonious relationship between U.S. and Canadian film industries—a new corporate reality that is progressive, productive, and, most importantly, profitable, as evidenced by the success of Canadian production communities such as Vancouver. By contrast, Americans laborers against so-called runaway production were framed as uninformed and distastefully protectionist of now-fluid cultural, economic, and geographic boundaries characteristic of the transnational and transcultural flow of the contemporary film industry.

A first manifestation of the pro-globalization discourse of runaway film production in the Canadian press relied on what Marwan Kraidy (2005) has described as "corporate transculturalism," or "a discourse in which fluid identities and porous cultural borders are depicted as growth engines in service of a cosmopolitan capitalism" (p. 90). Kraidy's concern was with the strategic deployment of discourses of hybridity—a highly contested concept that in its best use describes a continuum of experiences of the blending of cultural forms, and at its worst reinstates discourses of ethnic and racial purity. Thus, corporate transculturalism is viewed as an ethically questionable and profit-motivated use of the concept of hybridity, serving the needs of "a neoliberal economic order that respects no borders and harbors no prejudice toward cultural and ethnic difference that can be harnessed for growth" (p. 90).

One manifestation of corporate transculturalism in the Canadian runaway production debate was through "counterflow," referring to the infusion of diverse cultural representations within American-made media to appeal to non-U.S. audiences (Kraidy, 2005, p. 77). Within Canadian discussions of runaway film production, the argument was made that a Canadian cultural counterflow had become increasingly prevalent in mainstream U.S. media, particularly television. References to Canada in U.S. TV programs were used as evidence of the normalcy and mass marketability of the hybridization of Canadian and American cultures on the screen. Memorable examples include a *Montreal Gazette* review of an episode of the popular U.S. presidential drama *The West Wing* in which the author commented on the foregrounding of Canada in the storyline: one of the characters is informed that the north Minnesota border town in which she grew up had been re-zoned as part of Manitoba (Branswell, 2002). Throughout the article, the journalist speculated, along with the senior Canadian consulate in Los Angeles, that there must be Canadians working on the show's staff. Branswell was particularly thrilled that the show ended with the singing of "O, Canada." She offered this TV event as evidence of a latent "Canadianization" of Hollywood, despite "so-called runaway production" tensions: "What with all the anger over runaway productions, Canada isn't that popular in some TV and film circles in Los Angeles. But you'd never know it from watching *The West Wing*" (p. D6). The fact that 1.5 million Canadians watched the episode was offered as further proof of the overwhelming approval of the show's attempt at a culturally hybrid storyline, fitting neatly into the model of marketability inherent in discourses of corporate transculturalism.

Similarly, a case for Canadian counterflow was made regarding the growing number of Canadian actors "infiltrating" American television. An article in the *Toronto Star* provided a list of twenty-one Canadian-born actors starring in popular U.S. programs at the time of publication, including Eric McCormack of *Will & Grace*, Vanessa Lengies of *American Dreams*, Shaun Majumder of *Cedric The Entertainer*, and Gregory Smith of *Everwood* (More Canadians Invade, 2002). Canadian TV show host Jay Baruchel described the undetected Canadian "invasion" of Hollywood: "Bit by bit, we kind of get into the bloodstream of America. And because we're very similar, you don't know we're there. It's kind of like Invasion of the Body Snatchers. That's Canada. Body Snatchers and health care" (p. 11). Of note is the reversal in use of the "talent drain" argument previously made in the narrative of cultural imperialism. Here, the Canadian talent exodus to Los Angeles is used as a point of national pride, and as substantiation that Canadian actors have blended seamlessly into American-style television programs. The mention of "so-called runaway film production" in tandem with the actor story seems to have been an effort to show that cultural blurring has happened on multiple levels in the industry, regardless of whether some U.S. film workers are willing to admit it or not. And the fact that these actors had appeared on some of the most popular U.S. shows alongside famous U.S. talent was used to demonstrate further that hybridity was highly marketable.

During this time, the Screen Actors Guild of America was more concerned with the luring of its members to foreign locations under dubious conditions than Canadian counterflow through Hollywood. In 2001, the Guild began a campaign to enforce its already-existing "Global Rule One," which explicitly barred its members from working on non-union, nonsignatory projects staged in foreign locations. Past enforcement of the rule was patchy at best. In what seemed to be an elevated climate of economic runaway production, particularly to cheaper locales in Canada, the SAG felt it needed to be particularly vigilant about getting its members to abide by the rule. According to 2001 Guild president Melissa Gilbert, SAG's health and pension funds had lost an estimated $23 million in contributions due to members working on nonunion runaway productions (McNary, 2001). During the contentious SAG presidential campaign in Spring 2002 between incumbent Gilbert and Valerie Harper, the issues of runaway Canadian productions, industry subsidies, and Global Rule One enforcement were front and center. Stephen Waddell of the Alliance of Canadian Cinema, Television, and Radio Artists (ACTRA) chided Harper, in particular, for what he perceived to be her anti-Canadian rhetoric. Again, taking up the banner of corporate transculturalism, Waddell lamented the accusations and assumptions he saw behind the SAG push to enforce Global Rule One:

> "It's the same mindset that's at play, where the Hollywood-based performer believes those jobs that used to be in Hollywood should always be in Hollywood. Those jobs now are being shared, quite properly, by other workers outside the United States getting what is our fair share" (Sokoloff, 2002, p. A3).

The themes of counterflow and pro-globalization also surfaced in the form of anti-protectionist rhetoric, where attempts at national "cultural gatekeeping" by Hollywood labor were dismissed as disruptive to the free and open flow of cultural products (Kraidy, 2005, p. 78). This approach was particularly salient in discussions of "so-called" runaway production in which Canadians responded to criticism over the re-creation of U.S. landscapes in Canada for TV and film productions such as *My Big Fat Greek Wedding* (2002), *The X-Files*, and *Brokeback Mountain* (2005). In a story about the impending production of a TV series set in Pasadena, California, but slated to film in Vancouver, Lynne McNamara (2001) chided those leveling the "runaway location" argument as hypocritical: "[F]olks, let's not forget, it's called show 'business.' They're shooting the show here because it's cheaper. Not because Vancouver looks anything like Pasadena. It doesn't" (p. B9). For McNamara, the commodification of culture was a two-way street. If the U.S. film industry could "invade" the cultural boundaries of Canada via the representation of its landscapes in film, then the Canadian industry also had the right to interpret U.S. national and cultural identities through similar representations. In this line of thinking, such boundary distinctions contradicted the realities of show "business."

Pro-globalization crept into political commentary as well, specifically within the California gubernatorial recall election of 2003 between Austrian actor and Republican candidate Arnold Schwarzenegger and incumbent Democrat Gray Davis. Schwarzenegger included the issue of runaway film production on his campaign platform, promising to push for competitive tax incentives to help revive California's ailing film industry (McCullough, 2003). The last film the actor was scheduled to appear in before potentially entering political office was *Terminator 3: Rise of the Machines* (aka *T3*; 2003). Although the US $170 million film was originally slated to shoot in Vancouver Film Studios, Schwarzenegger personally renegotiated its relocation to Los Angeles in what appeared to be an act of appeasement toward California's vehement anti-runaway lobby. In a campaign speech addressed to the California Chamber of Commerce, Schwarzenegger emphasized that he had invested several million dollars of his own money to move *Terminator 3* back to Los Angeles. As governor, he promised that he would be committed to bringing production work back to California (Knelman, 2003, p. A03).

Schwarzenegger's commitment to addressing California's stagnant film industry sent some tremors through the Canadian industry, but most reactions in the press ridiculed his economic protectionist agenda. Referring to rumors that Schwarzenegger had shaved money from his own substantial fee to keep *T3* in Los Angeles, Tom Adair of the British Columbia Council of Film Unions called it a one-time "patriotic pay cut" that he doubted other U.S. movie stars would be willing to take (McCullough, 2003, p. I1). Other critics also chose to downplay the *T3* incident, arguing that the distressed state of California's budget made any long-term attempts by Schwarzenegger to reclaim the state's ownership of the film industry doubtful: "Schwarzenegger is likely to find that political currents and a budget mess in Sacramento will limit him to cajoling and arm-twisting rather than serving up more concrete measures such as financial incentives" (Bates, J., 2003, p. D8).

Similar disdain for economic protectionist activities was expressed toward American grassroots labor groups such as the Film and Television Action Committee (FTAC) which, as discussed previously, actively organized anti-runaway rallies in the United States and lobbied for anti-runaway legislation before Congress. In 2007, the group claimed to have over 150,000 supporters, including several labor and government organizations (About the FTAC, 2007). One of the primary criticisms of the FTAC by the Canadian press was their singular focus on Canada as well as their seeming ignorance of the widespread global growth of film production.

Several articles appearing in Canadian trade and popular press critiqued the FTAC's position on "so-called" Canadian runaway production. Journalist Doug Saunders (2001) chronicled a visit to FTAC member Brent Swift's special effects workshop in Los Angeles. In an ironic twist, Swift had been hired to construct and blow up a model of a downtown Vancouver high rise for a U.S.-produced action film. While the circumstances of the project seemed to support Swift's view that many Canadian-based productions could be shot in Los Angeles, Saunders emphasized that it was all a matter of perspective, and not necessarily a shared reality: "North of the border, you won't hear the phrase 'runaway productions,' though. The preferred term is 'Hollywood North,' and the favored myth has to do with American money creating a Canadian industry" (p. 94). In an article entitled "Production to Runaway Beyond Canada," *Playback* journalist Ian Edwards (2002) also provided a critique of FTAC's protectionist mission, pointing out that Canada was just one of many countries competing for Hollywood production work and providing competitive subsidies, including Australia, France, and Bulgaria (p. 10).

Both Saunders and Edwards perceived an increasing value of corporate transnational flow over the patrolled cultural and economic boundaries of the anti-runaway activists in the U.S. film industry. Inherent within the argument of counterflow was a commitment to processes of economic mobility and cultural fluidity via commodification. By contrast, the narrative of runaway film production and economic protectionism espoused by Arnold Schwarzenegger and the FTAC were rooted in cultural and industrial stasis—antiquated, divisive, and unrealistic ideals, in the opinion of some Canadians. Of course, there is a measure of hypocrisy in Edwards's position, given that Canada's film industry success was primarily built on cultural protectionist measures instituted within NAFTA and other trade agreements with the United States

But the point stands that the Canadian film industry felt justified in its use of industry incentives so they could be globally competitive—and they were not the only country offering such incentives on the global market.

A final connection between runaway film production and the theme of pro-globalization was found in Canadian press discussions of "co-production," in which the boundaries of labor relations between Canada, the United States, and other countries were blurred: workers at all levels, both "above" and "below-the-line," regardless of nationality, were described as working on common ground and toward common goals on so-called Canadian runaway projects. Anti-runaway discourse, by contrast, was framed as discordant and antithetical to a globalized film industry. A prime example was found in a *Playback* article in which the author responded to controversial statements by the FTAC that had drawn comparisons between the movement of September 11 terrorists across the Canadian border and the migration of film productions between Canada and the United States, Yaffe (2002, March) responded that such rhetoric was antithetical to building international "synergies" in the production industries, and that it was time for Canada to seek out new co-production partnerships in emerging markets, like New Zealand (p. 4).

Some Canadian industry experts emphasized the way co-production, as opposed to the stagnant, monolithic production environment of Hollywood, reinvigorated the film production process. A producer from the Canadian-based *X-Men* sequel observed that Canadian crews enjoyed the novelty of working on a big action film like *X-Men*, and that subsequently, the process was more energetic and collaborative than similar projects in Los Angeles (Monk, 2003, p. D3). By this logic, co-production and a transnational film industry model not only contributed to the overall economic fortitude of the industry, but also perhaps to its creative growth, in the breaking down of production routines, another trait which Negus & Román-Velázquez (2000) have attributed to discourses of pro-globalization.

In summary, positive constructions of globalization in the film industry and narratives of runaway film production employed several strategies to support their logic, including emphasizing the marketability of hybrid media production and content, castigating economic protectionism in Hollywood, and valorizing synergized multinational production teams. Each of these rhetorical strategies was inscribed with what Canclini (1995) has called the language of "de-territorialization," referring to "the loss of the 'natural' relation of culture to geographical and social territories" (p. 229). If filmmaking could be called a cultural practice, then "so-called" runaway production could be described as a process in which filmmaking had been dislodged from its territorial identification with Hollywood. Film and television productions could be successfully staged almost anywhere in the world, especially in Canada.

At the same time, the cultural composition of filmmaking in Hollywood was depicted as being in flux, with Canadians "infiltrating" and destabilizing its all-American image. However, as will be shown in the last narrative of "so-called" runaway production, the dislocation of cultural practices and identities from geography in processes of globalization can also result in discourses that celebrate and privilege the local.

The Narrative of Emancipation

Where there are claims to de-territorialization, discourses of "re-territorialization," or the reconstitution of cultural and geographic boundaries, will also be found (Canclini, 1995). This type of identity reinstatement is evident in the final thematic discourse of runaway film production found in Canadian press coverage—the narrative of emancipation. In these statements, Canadian film interests and journalists proposed a break from their service production relationship with the United States, arguing for a more self-sufficient and nationalistic industry. In many ways, this perspective represents the flip side of the narrative of cultural imperialism: the argument was made before that Canadian film workers had a right to participate in the production of U.S. media they had historically been forced to consume; the emancipatory discourse takes the next step, proposing that the Canadian film industry had the right and ability to produce and profit from the production of its own media on a national and international scale.

Canada's extensive production infrastructure and unique landscapes—both selling points for their service relationship with the United States—were reclaimed within the emancipation narrative as the very features that could make the country's domestic industry globally competitive. For instance, in a discussion of the international success of the Canadian independent film *Cube* (1997), actor David Hewlett—one of the film's stars—proposed "indie" filmmaking as an untapped market in Canada. Noting Canada's well-established infrastructure for productions, he reasoned, "We can make the little films that will make a ton of money. And I don't know why we don't" (Howell, 2001, p. 8).

Arnold Schwarzenegger's anti-runaway campaign also seemed to function as a lightning rod for emancipatory debates in the Canadian press. During this time, Canada's viability as an international, and not just American, film location was lauded by Samantha Yaffe (2002, January) in a *Playback* editorial. In short, Yaffe argued that Canada could weather any major reduction in American co-productions due to new tax incentives in the United States because Canada now had a reputation as a world-class production center, with massive soundstages and an impressive filmography including a long list of big-budget, blockbuster films (p. 4).

The second move toward emancipation offered by the Canadian trade press was the need to overcome Canada's historically constructed sense of inferiority to the United States in all manner of cultural and economic instances, including the motion picture and TV production industries. Opinion columnist Ken Ferguson of *Playback* outlined what he felt should be Canadian industry priorities for gaining confidence and independence, including the development of media that could appeal to audiences in Canada and beyond, and diversifying their interests by seeking out co-productions with countries other than the United States (Ferguson, 2005, p. 12). Similar comments regarding the development and legitimacy of the Canadian film industry were made by members of the production community in coverage of British Columbia's annual film and television industry awards—the Leos. As stated by Walter Daroshin, Leo Awards chairman, "We've grown from an industry of people who laid carpet and wound cable to a community of artists, and people who not only crew—but create, and even own the copyright to the property" (Monk, 2002, p. D7)

Emancipatory discourses in the Canadian press also emphasized the improved quality and marketability of domestically produced programs in comparison to those from the United States. In an interview regarding her award-winning documentary about Canadian tribute bands, *Mockstars*, filmmaker Michelle Welygan expressed her confidence in Canada's ability to produce appealing products, both culturally and aesthetically. By her estimation, the Canadian film and television industries had left behind their reputation for making cheap movies-of-the-week, and were now producing films with the same production quality as films made in Hollywood. (Monk, 2002, p. D7).

A crucial part of the emancipatory vision offered by Canadian journalists and film workers was a critique of their own industry and government's political actions toward building a strong domestic production sector. These statements typically focused on how the development and implementation of domestic policies by Canadian film unions and federal and provincial governments potentially frustrated Canada's efforts to become a global producer and distributor of media. For instance, Toronto producer Howard Rosen encouraged industry members to consider "the big picture" instead of short-term gains that might be garnered by limiting the number of work permits available to foreign talent: "As a producer of indigenous and service productions, my feeling is why waste time being the sneezing flea, why not find ways to be the mouse that roared?" (Rosen, 2001, p. 8). Ken Ferguson (2005) of *Playback* added his voice to those who questioned the way Canadian film subsidies were being used to support the historically unprofitable indigenous industry, perhaps at the expense of a sustainable, internationally competitive industry (p. 12).

Salient within all the emancipatory statements discussed in this section was a deeply embedded contradiction. On the one hand, there was a desire to become independent of the U.S. media industry, either by diversifying the Canadian industry's collaborations with foreign producers or by developing a strong, independent, commercially sustainable domestic industry. On the other hand, there was an acceptance that the Canadian film industry's independence was to some degree predicated on its ability to replicate the U.S. media's production methods and aesthetic at the expense of a unique Canadian product. Thus, the lines drawn between narratives of cultural oppression and emancipation were considerably blurred. Anthony McGrew (1996) has argued that such contradictions are inherent within discourses of globalization, accented by conflicting concepts such as centralization and decentralization, and homogenization and heterogenization. The narrative of emancipation in Canadian discussions of runaway film production both depends upon and runs counter to the narrative of cultural imperialism outlined previously, with the central contradiction being Canada's submission to the United States's cultural imperialist model for media production, consumption, and distribution as the means for emancipation. The masking of dependence on transnational investors such as the U.S. film industry is also an important part of the process of "production fetishism" (Appadurai,1996); though the Canadian film industry wanted to give the perception of having the political and economic wherewithal to stand on its own as a unique global media capital (Curtin, 2003), its dependence on Hollywood financing, management, and creative project development was always just under the surface.

Reverse Runaway Production

Despite the Canadian film community's many efforts to deconstruct and dismiss the discourse of runaway film production, they also employed the phrase to describe their own problems with migratory production and inter-provincial competition. As mentioned earlier, certain regions outside the popular Canadian production centers of Vancouver and Toronto began to offer their own "distant location" tax incentives in addition to those offered at the federal level, such as Saskatchewan and Manitoba. In the 2000s, many U.S. states also began to pass their own highly competitive tax incentives, including Louisiana, Michigan, and Illinois. For the latter, the tax credit is currently set at 30 percent of taxable production expenditures made in Illinois, and 30 percent of labor costs for Illinois workers—an incentive that many in the Chicago production community credit for landing the $100 million production of *Dark Knight* in 2008 (Illinois Department of Commerce and Equal Opportunity, 2009). Combined with a weakened U.S. dollar following the 9/11 attacks and the economic recession beginning in 2008, the economic edge long experienced by Canadian production was, to some degree, equalized. Other political and social factors have also been blamed for a decline in Canadian production, most notably the 2003 outbreak of Severe Acute Respiratory Syndrome (SARS) in Toronto. Subsequently, some Canadian film interests have lamented a "reverse" runaway production trend, with productions once guaranteed to flock to Vancouver or Toronto either locating in the United States, seeking deals in more far-flung Canadian locations, or globe trekking to other cheap foreign locations, such as New Zealand and Eastern Europe.

In 2002, concerns over a drop off in U.S. productions in Canada began to make their way into the trade press. Montreal production was down US$113 million from the previous year, while Toronto reported a noticeable drop in bigger budget TV movies-of-the-week (Kelly B., 2002, July). Expectations had been high that production would rebound in 2002 after a miserable 2001 production season, mostly blamed on prolonged Writers and Screen Actors Guild contract negotiations that temporarily halted production planning for fear of strikes, as well as the economic aftermath of the September 11 attacks. Toronto film commissioner Rhoda Silverstone suggested that the Canadian industry was, at least on some level, suffering from U.S. anti-runaway production backlash: "That's definitely going to have some effect. Some have decided to stay home because of the runaway production issue" (p. 14). Stephen Waddell, executive director of the 20,000-member Alliance of Canadian Cinema, Television and Radio Artists (ACTRA), echoed Silverstone's assessment by relaying a story about attending Cannes and witnessing American actors and journalists applauding Clint Eastwood for shooting *Mystic River* in Boston rather than Canada. Such incidents seemed to suggest that the public relations tide was starting to turn in the American industry's favor (MacDonald, 2003, p. R1).

But for Toronto, the U.S. campaign against runaway production was the least of their problems. In 2003, the World Health Organization placed the Ontario city on a watch list for SARS, having an immediate impact on the staging of U.S. productions there: the Jennifer Lopez film *Shall We Dance?* (2004) was quickly relocated to Winnipeg, while a remake of *The Goodbye Girl* moved to Vancouver (p. R1). Paul Kenyon, owner of a film locations services company in Toronto, expressed his frustration over the financial impact the SARS scare was having on his business: "SARS was completely irrational. We had a $750,000 loss as a result of SARS, and there hasn't been much to talk about since then" (Adams, 2004, p. R5). Overall, the estimated financial impact for Toronto's once-thriving film industry looked dire: U.S. production spending had dropped more than 40 percent from a high of $567 million in 2001 to $333 million in 2003 (Mitchell, 2004, p. D11). Ken Ferguson acknowledged the industry crisis created by the SARS scare, but felt that other issues were also contributing to Toronto's runaway production problems. Instead, Ferguson described a "perfect storm" of factors affecting Toronto's film industry, including a strengthening Canadian dollar, a trend toward low-cost reality TV production, and increased competition from other provinces (p. D11). "We have our own form of runaway productions where shows are going to Winnipeg and even the Yukon." Pointing out the lack of infrastructure in these remote locations, Ferguson added, "It makes no sense to us. But it probably makes no sense to the guys in L.A. when things come here" (Austen, 2004, p. 1).

Increased foreign competition also became a concern for Canadian film communities. Industry commentators took notice when New Zealand entered the spotlight after the overwhelming success of *The Lord of the Rings* trilogy in 2004. Several other high profile projects followed, including remakes of *The Last Samurai* (2003) and *King Kong* (2005). In a *Globe and Mail* article titled "Runaway Film Work Running Away," business reporter Eric Reguly (2004) expressed confusion over New Zealand's success. Given the remote location of the country and its lack of infrastructure compared to Canada, Reguly argued that, "The thought of anyone spending 15 hours on a plane to make a film on a South Pacific island was ridiculous" (p. B2). Many, including Reguly, blamed the work slippage on a move by the Canadian government in 2001 to remove one of the production tax shelters offered to foreign productions. The tax credit was later restored and even increased, but some felt it had knocked them out of the game. Don Carmody, an L.A.-based producer of the Toronto-made Oscar winner *Chicago* (2002), admitted that times had changed and that the film would more than likely have been made in New York in 2004 (the time of the interview) than Toronto due to new tax incentives offered by the state. He also saw competitive production centers emerging in Eastern Europe, with high profile Hollywood projects like Anthony Minghella's *Cold Mountain* (2003) shooting most of its schedule in Romania. Carmody admitted owning a home in Toronto to stay close to work there, but wondered aloud, "Maybe I had better sell it and buy a house in Bucharest" (Austen, 2004, p. 1).

Fears over reverse runaway production once again resurfaced within the Canadian film and television industries in 2007, with the beginning of the U.S. economic recession. One of the major selling points for attracting productions to Canada had been the favorable exchange rate. But in September 2007, the U.S. and Canadian dollars reached parity for the first time in thirty-one years (CDN$1= US$1: Loonie Reaches Parity, 2007), sending waves of panic through Canada's media production communities. As one production company owner in Montreal lamented, "The gossip within the American industry will be—why go to Canada?" (Kelly B., 2007, p. B2). With the onset of the Writers Guild strike in November 2007, Ontario, Quebec, and British

Columbia quickly boosted their provincial incentives by as much as 7 percent to keep their existing work from running away back to the United States (Kelly B., 2008). But despite the incentive increases, 2008 was a miserable year for Canadian production, with Toronto's industry reportedly making $79 million in U.S. productions that year, compared to $287 million in 2007 (Jowett, 2009, p. A11).

To make matters worse, many U.S. states also began augmenting their own anti-runaway film industry subsidies. In 2008, Michigan instituted a 40 percent tax credit covering a broad spectrum of film and television production expenses, including the bloated salaries of key actors (Paul, 2009). And in March 2009, Governor Schwarzenegger signed a tax incentive bill guaranteeing $100 million subsidy for below-the-line labor costs on California film and television projects, the first such subsidy bill to pass in the state (Wood, 2009, p. 3). Though U.S. and Canadian currencies were still close to parity in the summer of 2010 (US$1 to CDN$.99), reverse runaway production concerns began to subside as productions in Toronto rebounded by more than 40 percent over their 2009 figures (Singleton, 2010, p. 35). For some, the rebound of the Canadian industry was proof of their enduring reputation as a quality production labor force—something that would stand the test of time and continue to attract U.S. and other foreign producers, regardless of exchange rates. While others saw the rebound as primarily the result of the willingness of Canadian governments, both federal and provincial, to up the ante and increase production tax credits. As an executive officer of the Directors Guild of Canada British Columbia Council warned, "The dollar's the least of our worries. They've [U.S. producers] become accustomed to the fact that it's not going back to 72 cents. A U.S. dollar is a U.S. dollar here and in Michigan. The issue will be what the bigger production incentive will be" (Bradshaw, 2010, p. R5). Now, everyone was playing the industry subsidy game. And the only way to reverse the flow of so-called runaway productions, from either side of the border, would be to continue to raise the stakes and increase—an ominous prospect.

This final thematic category of Canadian runaway production illustrates a troublesome trend in the regionalization of film labor as observed by Susan Christopherson (2005): the more divided and localized production labor becomes, the better it is for multinational media corporations attempting to negotiate the best deal among dispersed, competitive global production communities. As in other globalized industries, the power of union contracts is typically undermined by such practices, where labor groups and their complicit state and federal governments are forced into a "race to the bottom"—matching and undermining each other's industry tax incentives and labor contracts to attract any production dollars they can in the short term.

As has been demonstrated throughout the history of runaway film production in the United States, competition for production work has not been limited to the national level. Rather, city, state, and in the Canadian case, provincial level competition has been commonplace. In a sense, the Canadian film industry's desire to be a player on a global scale had been realized. But with their elevation to the status of global media center came the uncertainty of the transnational deck being reshuffled in favor of another global media center—perhaps Bucharest or Boston—depending on the most favorable political and economic conditions at any given time.

CONCLUSION

The 1990s and early 2000s were a period of increased public consciousness and scrutiny of processes of globalization, with more open public debate regarding unbalanced free trade pacts, predatory multinational corporations, cultural imperialism, and labor outsourcing. Both U.S. and Canadian discourses of runaway film production have reflected these political, cultural, and economic shifts, with each constructing themselves as victims—and sometimes benefactors—of a globalizing film industry. From an American perspective, film workers in Hollywood and across the country have been victims of loopholes built into the North American Free Trade Agreement, allowing Canada to institute anti-competitive industry subsidies to lure away American jobs. From a Canadian perspective, negotiated cultural exemptions, industry subsidies, and so-called runaway productions are merely correctives for decades of American cultural imperialism, particularly through media trade.

Interestingly, the competing perspectives of U.S. and Canadian film communities represent both the disjunctures and compatibilities between economic and cultural agendas in a globalizing industry. On the one hand, industry trade groups such as the Motion Picture Association of America have consistently opposed the notion of defining the U.S. film industry as a cultural industry in need of subsidies and protections as Canada has done. Such definitions have been viewed by the MPAA and its constituency as ultimately hindering free trade policies—policies that treat film and media products strictly as commodities competing in a global free market, and consistently favor the United States (e.g., Crabtree, 2004; DiOrio, 2001; Pollock, 1984). And yet as we see in the Canadian case, Hollywood producers and above-the-line interests have greatly benefitted from the cultural subsidies and industry protections instituted by Canadian federal and provincial governments. As was shown in the Canadian responses to runaway film production, the disjuncture between American global capitalism and Canadian cultural protectionism has been bridged by the ideology of corporate transculturalism (Kraidy, 2005), where the definition of culture itself can be manipulated and put into the service of a capitalist agenda.

Though emphasis has been placed on the competing national discourses of runaway film production in the 1990s and early 2000s, there is also much evidence demonstrating how the global film industry transcends the nation-state. Labor interests were being regionalized in both the United States and Canada: Hollywood was being pitted against Vancouver, New York, and Chicago production communities; Chicago was competing with Toronto, and Toronto competing with Montreal and Vancouver, etc. In this sense, the 1990s and 2000s represent a point where runaway production was becoming more recognizable as a rhizomatic construct—a tangle of multi-vocal, transhistorical, but interrelated discourses (Duara, 1996; Malkki, 1996). But this is not to suggest sympathy or harmony among those dispersed production communities in the United States and Canada activating the concept of runaway production on their own behalf. Rather than working together to create common standards and stability for organized labor within the New International Division of Cultural Labor, international film unions such as the International Alliance of Theatrical and Stage Employees are beset with infighting and turf battles amongst their own locals—locked in a classic "race to the bottom" in their efforts to compete for production dollars (Christopherson, 2005). State, provincial, and federal governments are arguably complicit in this process, scrambling to create the most attractive subsidy package and become the next favorite runaway location.

NOTE

1. Portions of this chapter were first published in the following article, and appear in this book courtesy of Taylor & Francis (www.tandfonline.com): Johnson-Yale, C. (2008). "So-Called Runaway Film Production": Countering Hollywood's Outsourcing Narrative in the Canadian Press. *Critical Studies in Media Communication*, *25*(2), 113–134. doi:10.1080/15295030802032259.

Conclusion

Runaway film production has been with us for nearly seventy years. In its most basic form, this discourse has been used by Hollywood and U.S. film labor to describe the outsourcing of production to less expensive non-U.S. locations. But as this history has shown, runaway production is a discourse with multiple meanings, dependent upon shifting and overlapping political, economic, and cultural variables. In the 1940s and 1950s, runaway production described film labor as a bargaining chip within U.S.–European postwar politics. In the 1960s, McCarthyism was combined with runaway production to frame Hollywood's elite as un-American deviants "running" to Europe for political and economic exile. In the 1970s and 1980s, runaway production was once again re-imagined to describe domestic and regional competition for production dollars. And finally, in the 1990s and 2000s, runaway production has been folded into continuing debates over globalization and free trade practices, emboldening production communities like Vancouver labeled as runaway locations to challenge the protectionist sentiments embedded within the phrase.

On the surface, the multiple meanings applied to runaway production over time seem discordant, switching back and forth over the decades between cultural, political, and economic causes and implications. But as Stuart Hall (1996) explains, discourses are comprised of groups of statements that "provide a language for talking about—i.e., a way of representing—a particular kind of knowledge about a topic" (p. 201). They actively produce and limit our understandings of issues, and in some instances, force us into a particular worldview, even if we are consciously opposed to it, as in Hall's critique of the discourse of "the West and the rest." Similarly, the multiple and often contradictory statements that have comprised the discursive formation of runaway production have provided a language and framework for understanding globalizing media industries. Specifically, the discourse has attempted to reinforce the natural superiority of Hollywood (and sometimes more broadly, the United States) as the "authentic" home of motion picture and television production while constructing all other competing production communities as the naturally inferior, criminal harborers of Hollywood's "runaways." Locations as far-ranging as Europe and Australia, and as close as San Francisco and Mexico, have all been constructed at some point in the history of runaway production as less authentic than Hollywood, no matter their histories as film production communities outside their relationship with Hollywood. And despite Canada's best efforts to question the validity of the discourse of runaway production, they also have fallen into the discursive trap described by Hall, where they have been forced to respond to runaway accusations within the worldview of "Hollywood and the rest." For better or worse, Hollywood has been the yardstick against which Canada and other production centers have been made to measure themselves. And the discourse of runaway film production has only worked to reinforce this Hollywood-centric subject position.

Of course, the argument could (and has) been made that there is some truth in the discourse of runaway production; that Hollywood represents the industrial home of global film production, and like many other globalizing production hubs (e.g., Detroit) their labor have increasingly suffered the effects of outsourcing. But as Hall has contended, the truth or falsehood of such a discourse is often difficult to prove, and is in many ways secondary to its ability to *function* as truth. The manipulation of language in discourse can shift perceptions so that something that seems false can be "*made* 'true' because people act on them believing that they are true." Subsequently, "it is power, rather than the facts about reality, which make things 'true'" (Hall, 1996, p. 203). In the many variations of the discourse of runaway production discussed in this history, the facts that support the phenomenon have constantly been in flux: runaway locations, political and economic motivations of "runaways," Hollywood unemployment figures, U.S. lost revenue figures, etc., have continually been proposed, contested, and reconstructed since 1949 when the discourse came into use. But regardless of the actual truth or falsehood of runaway production, it is *made* true by the fact that people have been compelled to respond to it and act upon it. Labor groups, legislators, journalists, and even academics have all in some way contributed to the "truth" of runaway production as an outsourcing phenomenon by writing numerous articles about the issue, organizing public rallies against it, and proposing and sometimes passing legislation to end the practice.

It could also be argued that time itself has contributed to the "truthfulness" of runaway film production—both its endurance as an independent discourse, as well as its relationship to the historical archive of neoliberal supra-discourses, including globalization and the "manifest destiny" of global free trade. As du Gay (2000) has explained, "the concept of 'globalization' has achieved such widespread exposure and has become such a powerful explanatory device and guide to action that it sometimes appears almost unquestionable" (p. 115). Likewise, the "unquestionable" and inevitable nature of the discourse of globalization has served as both an explanatory device and a point of opposition within debates over runaway film production: Hollywood and U.S. labor argued for legislation to help control the effects of globalization on production workers, while their opposition has argued the inevitability of global free trade and labor outsourcing. In either instance, the discourse of runaway production has been bolstered and reified by its association with the discourse of globalization—one of the most powerful economic discourses in terms of its ability to incite action and *re*-action on an international scale.

RUNAWAY PRODUCTION AS A HEGEMONIC DISCOURSE

Accepting the multiplicity and ambiguity of runaway production as a historical discourse, two questions arise: how and why has the discourse endured? Runaway film production was a discourse that originated among labor, with labor's interests in mind. It was meant to highlight the injustice of production labor outsourcing for an industry that had been, up to that point, almost entirely geographically bound to Hollywood. And yet when examining the history of runaway film production, it is questionable whether the discourse has been effective in garnering public sympathy and support for Hollywood and U.S. film labor, or whether it has served as an effective platform for anti-outsourcing legislation. Hall (1996) has explained that a common discourse can be used by different groups with disparate, even directly conflicting, class interests (p. 203). And so, it would appear to be the case with runaway production where, despite labor's seeming intention to challenge existing power and class relations in the Hollywood film industry, history demonstrates that it has more often functioned to reinforce the existing power structure.

From the frozen funds production debates of the 1940s and 1950s to the Canadian subsidies debates of the 1990s and 2000s, anti-runaway production efforts have resulted in several measures that have ultimately benefited transnational media corporations, including union concessions and state level tax credits. These same anti-runaway policies have also empowered runaway producers to pit localized film labor communities against one another by encouraging each to come up with a more competitive production incentive package than the next; a "divide and conquer" strategy that has eroded union solidarity and collective bargaining power amongst union film labor, particularly for the International Alliance of Theatrical and Stage Employes (Christopherson, 2005). Labor and industry subsidies meant to stop runaway film production have inadvertently reframed the problem as one of labor and supposedly bloated labor costs. Time and time again, "runaway" producers and directors defended their collaboration with non-union labor as their only recourse when faced with exorbitant union wages in Hollywood, most memorably in cases involving union extras and union animators. And in nearly all instances, union labor capitulated to the producers' and directors' demands; even the Hollywood animators' landmark "runaway clause" was eventually excised from their contract in exchange for wage increases (that they were likely already owed). This labor-oriented construction of runaway production has conveniently taken the focus away from owners and producers and other aspects of production under their control that have impacted film budgets perhaps even more than below-the-line labor costs, including increasingly extravagant transmedia marketing strategies, elaborate digital effects, and bloated above-the-line salaries (Wasko, 2003, p. 47).

Arguably, the history of runaway production tells the tale of the shaping of Hollywood labor into "governable" subjects within the New International Division of Cultural Labor. In the beginning, the discourse of runaway production represented a challenge to the dominant political and economic structures of the Hollywood film industry: labor attempted to exert their will and "bring Hollywood home" through disciplinary actions, such as lobbying for the repeal of the 18-month tax rule and labeling runaway actors and directors as un-American. But by the 1970s, we began to see runaway production as a rallying cry for industry-friendly policies; policies that, as explained before, tended to focus on solving the "problem" of union labor costs through corporate-friendly tax credits for labor.

In summary, the discourse of runaway film production has better served the hegemonic interests of those controlling the New International Division of Cultural Labor (NICL)—producers, directors, studios and other production owners—than the interests of below-the-line production labor. According to Miller et al. (2001), labor oppression is inherent within the NICL, characterized by a careful balance between "labor productivity, exploitation, and social control," coordinated by multinational corporations and various government entities (pp. 120–21). But rather than disrupt the cycle of oppression and exploitation instituted by the NICL, runaway film production seems only to have exaggerated its effects. As evidenced in the case of the IATSE, the discourse of runaway film production has reinforced the localizing and compartmentalizing of labor across the NICL: it is a discourse of geographically-bounded economic protectionism, perfectly compatible with the free trade, free market values of corporate Hollywood that thrive on market competition. While the goal of unions is to create some stability in the value of labor through collective bargaining, the isolation and destabilization of film labor locals through the discourse of runaway film production and within the NICL makes film labor no different than any other commodity on the open market. In many ways, the discourse of runaway film production has only worked to highlight the vulnerability of below-the-line labor within the NICL, particularly their lack of mobility within, and control over, the political, economic, and cultural "scapes" of transnational media industries (Appadurai, 1996).

Runaway Production, the State, and Cultural Patrimony

The hegemonic nature of the discourse of runaway production may also be related to the conditions of governmentality that have existed within the Hollywood film industry itself. As defined by Bratich, Packer and McCarthy (2003), governmentality is "the arts and rationalities of governing, where the conduct of conduct is the key activity" (p. 4). Rather than being the sole domain of the State, "the conduct of conduct takes place at innumerable sites, through an array of techniques and programs that are usually defined as cultural" (p. 4). As one of these cultural sites, the Hollywood production industry has functioned as an ideal instrument of governmentality, both in terms of the products produced as well as its function as an industry. In short, Hollywood films and media products have provided a way for people to reflect on themselves as "governed" subjects, particularly in regards to prevailing "morals, manners, and ways of life" (Bennett, 1992, p. 26). This theme was particularly prevalent in the runaway production debates in the 1940s through 1960s, when producers, directors, and leaders of the MPAA justified the production of American narrative films in foreign countries as emissaries for democracy in the politically and economically vulnerable countries of postwar Europe. On an industry level, Hollywood film production has provided an ideal model of Western economic liberalism: a mobile, self-governing industry that maintains its regulatory independence by proselytizing U.S. free market values (Packer, 2003). This was also a popular argument during the Cold War era of runaway production, when Eric Johnston and Jack Valenti argued the value of staging Hollywood productions in countries in danger of Communist takeover, to show the "American Way" of working and doing business.

The importance of the state in perpetuating the hegemony of global Hollywood is also evident within the runaway subsidy debates, where its role appears to go beyond controlling industry resources to commodifying cultural heritage. As previously explained, there is a coordination and collusion between various interests within the NICL, most particularly between transnational media interests and the state (Appadurai, 1996; Miller, et al., 2001). The story of runaway production corroborates this model, but also makes clear that one of the most important contributions that the state has made to global Hollywood is its ability to institutionalize definitions of culture that best serve the political and economic needs of industry owners, and by default, the interests of the state. I would also argue that the history of runaway production requires us to look beyond international trade activities and policies, the primary focus within most analyses of global Hollywood and runaway production, and consider the way that local, regional, provincial and state governments are also constructing and commodifying cultural meaning in the service of the NICL.

Tony Bennett (1992) has argued that within systems of state power, culture is not treated as an object of government, or a "subversive opposite" of government, but rather as "an instrument of government . . . to be applied in the service of government" (p. 25). More specifically, Bennett has defined culture as:

> [A] historically specific set of institutionally embedded relations of government in which the forms of thought and conduct of extended populations are targeted for transformation—in part via the extension through the social body of the forms, techniques, and regimens of aesthetic and intellectual culture. (pp. 26–27)

While Bennett used the public museum as his subject for understanding the role of cultural institutions in transforming the "thoughts and conduct" of the public on behalf of government, he also considered the question of cultural trade policies and the case of government-mandated film quotas and industry subsidies in Australia and Canada. He noted the peculiarities and pitfalls of trying to define "Australianness" within policy language for the sake of applying industry subsidies: How would "Australianness" be explicated in terms of film production finance? And in terms of film aesthetics, would "Australianness" automatically be assumed to be the caricatured and seemingly more "authentic" Outback Australia, or would urban aspects also be folded into the landscape of Australia's cultural film policy initiatives?

In the history of runaway production, we see the struggle to define cultural meaning and authenticity predicted by Bennett played out between media owners, labor, and the state. On the one hand, it appears to be the case that media industry owners have historically had more influence than labor at national and international levels. In the United States, these industry owners, represented by the MPAA, have effectively blocked efforts to subsidize the film industry as a cultural industry by arguing the importance of maintaining a commodity structure in support of global free trade. Alternately, Canadian industry interests, in association with the Department of Canadian Heritage, have fought for a cultural definition for their media, successfully negotiating cultural exemptions in its major free trade negotiations with the United States, specifically the GATT and NAFTA. And as discussed in chapter 5, these exemptions have been key in justifying national level film and television industry subsidies.

Clearly in each case, the state has played an important role in defining culture in relation to, and through, their respective media industries. But it is also evident that these decisions have ultimately fallen out in favor of hegemonic interests, namely the Hollywood studios. Canadian subsidies for their indigenous industry were instituted to create a more cohesive Canadian cultural identity. And yet, these same subsidies have seemingly served to further commodify their cultural identity within the New International Division of Cultural Labor, as they have become increasingly focused on flexible "corporate transculturalism" (Kraidy, 2005) and Hollywood investment. In turn, the "authentic" meaning of Canadianess has been reduced to a pragmatic set of constructs that can be easily defined and practically applied within industry subsidies, e.g., quotas for Canadian-identified labor in various sectors of production. In the United States, the MPAA's free trade agenda has fit seamlessly with that of the state, while at the same time the state has given its blessing to Hollywood's ownership class to play the cultural subsidy game in other countries to engender good will and ultimately break down such cultural protectionist practices.

Film labor interests, on the other hand, have more effectively appealed to municipal and state level legislators to help create anti-runaway production policies, often in response to national level subsidies in other countries such as England and Canada. This has included efforts by the Los Angeles and California Film Commissions to simplify the location permit process, and more recently, the surge in state-level subsidies across the country in places like Illinois and Louisiana. Much like the cultural subsidies in Canada, municipal and state policies in the United States have functioned to define and protect unique, geographically-specific (if not culturally-specific) workforces. But this has also meant that, like Canada, the cultural identity of labor has been reduced to a set of practical criteria to be met by a visiting production, e.g., tax credits that apply only to Louisiana labor costs. In this sense, there seems to be a direct correlation between the devaluing of labor via subsidies, and the devaluing of their cultural identity: to Hollywood producers, labor in places like Canada, Louisiana, and New Zealand share one important identity—that of inexpensive labor. And no other set of institutions has been more instrumental in commodifying the cultural identity of production labor than the state.

RUNAWAY PRODUCTION AND THE SHIFTING SPATIALITIES OF MEDIA LABOR

The discourse of runaway film production and the development of a New International Division of Cultural Labor might also be argued to represent a more general, historical shift in the spatial construction of labor. Organized labor groups are, by their very nature, preoccupied with territoriality. This is evident in the language that unions use to identify themselves: regional chapters of unions call themselves "locals," as in Chicago's IATSE Local 476, or Hollywood's IATSE Local 33. The identification of Locals can also be used to mark out union "turfs" within a market, e.g., Chicago IATSE Local 2, representing stagehands for the city's theaters and concert venues, and Local 476, representing Chicago film and television production labor. Though located in the same city, few hold memberships in both Locals. Territoriality is also evident in organized labor's focus on jurisdictions. Unions are constantly in the process of trying to expand and reinforce their jurisdiction over workers in specific geographic regions, in specific industries, and in specific workplaces.

Given organized labor's dependence on spatial definitions, we can begin to see the history of runaway film production as an extended, discursive reaction to the systematic deterritorialization of labor begun in the 1940s and 1950s. The introduction of runaway film production into the Hollywood union lexicon was prefaced by the jurisdictional battle in Hollywood between IATSE and the Conference of Studio Unions (CSU). And as discussed in chapter 1, many other policies and events followed that greatly restricted the ability of Hollywood unions to maintain jurisdiction over their industry: the passing of the Taft-Hartley Act (1947), the General Agreement on Tariffs and Trade (GATT, 1949), the disbanding of the studio system (1948), and the opening of European markets after World War II trough the Marshall Plan (1947), to name a few. And certainly, with all the changes that were being instituted at the time that were meant to hem in the spatial authority of Hollywood labor, and organized labor more generally, it must have truly felt like their industry and work was "running away."

The sense of spatial disruption experienced among organized labor, both inside and outside Hollywood, seems only to have increased in the 1990s and 2000s. As the historical progression of the discourse of runaway production demonstrates, and as many scholars of global media industries have argued (Appadurai, 1996; Curtin, 2003; Miller, Govil, McMurria, & Maxwell, 2001; Morley, 2001; Mosco, 2006; Schiller, 2000), the primacy of the nation-state has been gradually challenged and deteriorated by the rise of powerful multinational corporations. Arguably, we see this trend mirrored in union involvement in anti-runaway efforts, as international and national union representation have gradually over the last seventy years turned over anti-runaway production efforts to state and regional labor interests, including state and municipal film commissions and regional lobbying groups like Hollywood's Film and Television Action Committee.

And yet, the discourse of runaway production reveals another layer of labor de-territorialization, as Hollywood unions have fought to retain some ownership over what constitutes "Hollywood" production in a transnationalizing industry. As many industry scholars have observed (Bordwell, Staiger & Thompson, 1985; Miller, et al., 2001; Wasko, 2008), Hollywood has evolved over the last 100 years from being a "place" where production occurs, to an exportable production process. I would take this argument one step further to suggest that the history of runaway production has shown Hollywood to be more than an exportable process, but rather an exportable production "space." As described by Meaghan Morris (1988), space is the product of the transformation of place, and not the substance of place; space "occurs" and is composed of intersections of mobile elements—"space is a practiced place." Hollywood would seem to be the epitome of "practiced place": the production practices and routines of Hollywood the "place" distilled into a mobile, ephemeral experience of labor. And if space is productive, as James Hay (2003) and Henri LeFebvre (1991) have argued, labor working within this space necessarily becomes its product—in this instance, it becomes Hollywood labor. Therefore, as an expression of the spatial disruption of film labor, the discourse of runaway film production becomes more than just a lament over the loss of production work to locations outside geographic Hollywood; it becomes a lament over the loss of a spatialized and previously privileged labor identity—one that can be easily reproduced, and exploited, within the multiple and dispersed spaces of global Hollywood.

Finally, this brings us to the issue of labor mobility as expressed within the historical discourse of runaway film production. As argued by Massey (1984) and Miller, et al. (2001), the global and/or regional movement of labor is predicated upon their relation to the flows of capital and political power within the New International Division of Cultural Labor: those with more power over political and economic flows tend to have more agency within the NICL, while those with little influence tend to be at its mercy. The history of the discourse of runaway production repeatedly demonstrated this dynamic, as above-the-line labor interests, including producers, directors, and movie stars, were able to exercise control over the investment of production dollars in "runaway" locations, as well as influence industry-friendly economic policies on local, regional, and international scales—Elizabeth Taylor could force investment in overseas production by insisting on working abroad, while

Arnold Schwarzenegger could redirect the flow of capital back to Los Angeles at will in order to "bring Hollywood home." This control over the flow of capital and political power has also meant that above-the-line production labor has been more mobile within the NICL; they are the "runaways" who have travelled alongside transnational capital investments, and they are the architects and keepers of the transnational Hollywood "ideoscape"—the emissaries of global capitalism in international trade agreements and the faces of democracy and all-Americanism in the "runaway" media products produced.

Alternately, below-the-line labor's (e.g., lighting technicians, wardrobe attendants, carpenters, extras, etc.) mobility has been shown to be greatly limited throughout the history of runaway production, along with their ability to influence the movement of capital and development of economic policies within the NICL. On a federal level, labor opponents of runaway production practices have been given an audience with government officials, but rarely have these meetings resulted in actual policy initiatives, let alone binding legislation. Labor has had more success influencing anti-runaway policies at the local and regional level, though these efforts have had little long-term impact on the flow of production investment to Hollywood or other U.S. production centers, or on the construction of these localized labor forces as mobile. But as previously discussed, the lack of agency and mobility of Hollywood labor within the NICL has not precluded the commodification and mobility of the Hollywood labor *identity* on the global free market. In this sense, the history of runaway production is the history of the development of a Hollywood labor diaspora, with Los Angeles as its mythic and nostalgic homeland, back to which Hollywood's wayward "runaways" may someday return.

THE FUTURE OF RUNAWAY PRODUCTION

As Hollywood production has continued to globalize, and so-called runaway locations like Vancouver have sustained their success and proven their legitimacy as global production centers, several questions arise: Has the discourse of runaway production run its course? Can Hollywood and U.S. film labor continue to make charges of runaway production in an industry defined by political, economic, and cultural mobility? Is the trend toward Hollywood filmmaking heavily dependent on post-production visual effects (i.e., *Avatar* [2009], *Harry Potter and the Deathly Hollows* [2010]) making the issue of production labor outsourcing and runaway production irrelevant, or perhaps obsolete?

The seventy-year history depicted in this book stands as a testament to the resilience of the discourse of runaway production. Regardless of its accuracy in describing unemployment issues in Hollywood, or production labor competition domestically and abroad, it has a momentum and usefulness as a lobbying device. This is evident in the Hollywood trade and mainstream press, where runaway production continues to make regular appearances. With the U.S. economy in recovering from recession, and state film industry tax credits under increased scrutiny, the argument could be made that the rhetorical power of runaway production as a cultural and economic discourse could become even more potent.

Runaway film production is also finding new life within global production communities dubbed "runaway locations" themselves. As described in chapter 4, the discourse of runaway production has cropped up among labor in Canada's major production hubs, Toronto and Vancouver, as other Canadian cities and their provinces have created industry subsidies and made their play for Hollywood production dollars. In some instances, we now see non-U.S. production locations adopting the identification of "runaway location" to declare their position as a community willing to negotiate steep incentives to attract Hollywood producers. This was the case in New Zealand, where their production industry became a pawn in a battle between Australian unions and Hollywood producers over the labor contract for the much-anticipated *Lord of the Rings* prequel, *The Hobbit*. Production interests in New Zealand were proud of their success as a runaway location, but also had to come to terms with the tenuous nature of that success as their fate hinged on whether their government would institute policies to keep unions out of their industry to appease Warner Bros. (Editorial: Losing the Plot in "Hobbit" Row, 2010). So, contrary to the notion that the globalizing of Hollywood has somehow normalized mobile production practices and neutralized the discourse of runaway production, I would argue that the opposite is true: Continuing expansion and development of the NICL has only intensified competition and the sense of industry ownership among locations now deeply invested in maintaining some relationship with Hollywood.

Finally, I am unconvinced that increasing dependence on computer-based film production practices will spell the end of labor disputes and runaway production complaints. Again, one need only look at the runaway problems of *The Hobbit* in New Zealand to see that even films heavily dependent on visual effects are often still very dependent on human actors and crew to bring the characters to life and create a realistic atmosphere. Films that are mostly comprised of visual effects also tend to have much higher budgets than their live action counterparts: in 2009, live-action Oscar winner *The Hurt Locker* had a budget of $15 million, while the visual effects extravaganza *Avatar* had a reported production budget of $237 million. Interestingly, both projects did some of their filming in well-known runaway locations: *The Hurt Locker* in

Vancouver, and *Avatar* in New Zealand. But clearly, the stakes were much higher for the producers of *Avatar* who faced a much steeper deficit to break even, and therefore had the most to gain by using budget-friendly "runaway" locations with generous tax incentives.

In short, despite impressive technological advances in filmmaking, it is still a process that requires the collaboration and skill of hundreds of people per project. Someone still needs to operate the camera, set the lights, hang the green screen, prepare meals for the crew, drive trucks, apply makeup, buy wardrobe, coordinate stunts, design sets, hand out props, so on and so forth. And as long as there remains a human element in filmmaking, with production jobs at stake, I am convinced that the discourse of runaway production will endure.

References

$1 CDN=$1 US: Loonie reaches parity. (2007, September 20). Retrieved October 4, 2010, from CBC News: http://www.cbc.ca/money/story/2007/09/20/canadiandol lar.html.

About the FTAC. (2007). Retrieved December 28, 2009, from Film and Television Action Committee: http://www.ftac.net/html/about.html.

Academy of Motion Picture Arts and Sciences. (2007). *Motion Picture Industry Council, Inc.: Biography/History.* Retrieved September 19, 2007, from Margaret Herrick Library: Academy of Motion Picture Arts and Sciences: http://www.os cars.org/mhl/hn/mpic_hn.html.

Action sought against British curb on films. (1949, March 29). *Los Angeles Times*, p. A8.

Actors Guild asks probe of filmmaking abroad. (1953, June 18). *Los Angeles Times*, p. 5.

Adams, J. (2004, December 1). Hollywood North seeks Ontario tax help. *The Globe and Mail*, p. R5, Business.

AFL Council to ask gov't act on films made abroad: Ready to request ban on exhib here. (1949, February 15). *Hollywood Reporter*, p. 14.

AFL Film Council intensifies drive on foreign production. (1959, September 23). *Hollywood Reporter.*

AFL Film Council reopens fight on 'runaway' films: Union leaders hit exodus to Mexico. (1955, August 12). *Hollywood Reporter*, p. 9.

AFL pressures beer, drug companies to drop telepix lensed abroad. (1953, January 30). *Variety*, pp. 1, 4.

AFL stiffens attitude on film production abroad. (1953, January 21). *Variety*, pp. 1, 14.

Allen, J. (1996). Fordism and modern industry. In S. Hall, D. Held, D. Hubert, & K. Thompson (Eds.), *Modernity: An introduction to modern societies* (pp. 280–306). Oxford, UK: Blackwell.

Alpert, D. (1961, December 10). Laurence Harvey a runaway? "Nonsense!" *Los Angeles Times*, p. Q10.

Alum Silverman directs "Simpsons Movie." (2007, August 7). Retrieved August 2, 2008, from UCLA School of Theater, Film and Television: http://www.tft.ucla.edu/news/press/385-ucla-magazine_david-silverman/.

Amendment of the Internal Revenue Code to eliminate the earned income exemption granted to American citizens present in a foreign country for 17 months, H.R. 4552, 83d Cong. (1953).

Amin, A. (1994). Post-Fordism: Models, fantasies and phantoms of transition, in Post-Fordism: A Reader. In Amin, A. (Ed.). *Post-Fordism: A reader* (pp. 1–39). Oxford, UK: Blackwell Publishers.

Appadurai, A. (1996). *Modernity at large.* Minneapolis: University of Minnesota Press.

Arthur, A. (1949, April 6). Memorandum regarding British screen quotas. Motion Picture Industry Council.

Assembly Committee on Economic Development and New Technologies. (1985). *Runaway film production and film production in nonmetropolitan areas.* Sacramento: Assembly California Legislature.

Austen, I. (2004, December 23). Fade to black in Canada's film work. *New York Times*, p. 1, Business.

B.C. Film Commission. (2010, February 28). *Tax incentives.* Retrieved February 28, 2010, from http://www.bcfilmcommission.com/production/tax_incentives.htm.

Balio, T. (1976). *The American film industry.* Madison: University of Wisconsin Press.

——— (1996). *Grand design: Hollywood as a modern business enterprise, 1930-1939.* Berkeley: University of California Press.

Bart, P. (1965, February 7). Union gains mean Hollywood's loss. *New York Times*, p. X7.

——— (1965, July 10). Increased Hollywood production leading to shortages in facilities. *New York Times*, p. 15.

Bates, J. (1987, November 15). A special report on the Southern California economy. *Los Angeles Times*, p. 14.

——— (2003, October 23). Arnie unlikely to terminate runaway TV, film projects. *Vancouver Sun*, p. D8, Business.

Bennett, T. (1992). Putting policy into cultural studies. In L. Grossberg, C. Nelson, & P. Treichler (Eds.), *Cultural studies* (pp. 23–37). New York: Routledge.

Bennett, T., Grossberg, L., Morris, M., and Williams, R. (Eds.) (2005). *New keywords: A revised vocabulary of culture and society.* Malden, MA: Blackwell.

Bernstein, H. (1979, August 16). Cartoonists defy union leader, continue strike. *Los Angeles Times*, p. B30.

——— (1982, August 30). Labor: For animators, policy is no laughing matter. *Los Angeles Times*, p. E1.

Bernstein, I. (1957, December). *Hollywood at the Crossroads: An economic study of the motion picture industry.* Hollywood: Hollywood AFL Film Council.

Bertrand, C. (1987). American cultural imperialism—a myth? *American Studies International, 25* (1), pp. 46–58.

Bewitched remains H'wood. (1971, April 30). *Hollywood Reporter*, p. 1.

Bielby, D., & Harrington, C. L. (2005). Opening America? The telenovela-ization of U.S. soap operas. *Television & New Media , 6*, 383–99.

Bordwell, D., Staiger, J., & Thompson, K. (1985). *The classical Hollywood cinema.* New York: Columbia University Press.

Bracken, L. (2004, October 25). Study shoots down runaway gripes. *Playback*, p. 1, News.

Bradshaw, J. (2010, April 10). Dollar's rise will have less of an impact, thanks to lessons learned. *Globe and Mail (Canada)*, p. R5.

Brady, T. (1949, February 20). Hollywood protest: Labor group advocates retaliatory ban on foreign films. *New York Times*, p. X5.

Branswell, H. (2002, March 9). Land of silver birch, home of Donna? *Montreal Gazette*, p. D6, Arts & Entertainment.

Bratich, J. Z., Packer, J., & McCarthy, C. (2003). Governing the present. In J. Z. Bratich, J. Packer, & C. McCarthy (Eds.), *Foucault, cultural studies, and governmentality* (pp. 3–22). Albany: State University of New York Press.

Braverman, H. (1974). *Labor and monopoly capital.* New York: Monthly Review Press.

Brewer Charles Lick protests AFL nix on foreign vidpix. (1953, February 9). *Variety*, p. 18.

Brewer lists 21 names as seeking tax-exempt assignments overseas. (1953, January 27). *Variety*, pp. 1, 11.

Brewer, R. (1948, July). Movies for labor: Hollywood Film Council leads the way. *American Federationist*, pp. 10–11, 35.

British Columbia Film Commission. (2010, July). *Industry Profile.* Retrieved July 23, 2010, from http://www.bcfilmcommission.com/about_us/industry_profile/articles44.php

Brown Jr., E. (1975, September 27). Senate Bill 1189 veto letter. Sacramento, CA.

Brown asked to veto bill slashing film tax. (1963, June 5). *Los Angeles Times*, p. 24.

Brown ponders bill on movie tax exemption. (1963, June 14). *Los Angeles Times*, p. 12.

Browning, N. L. (1968, November 13). Blame filming costs on stars. *Chicago Tribune*, p. B7.

Burgess, S. (1999, September 2). Upping the ante in Hollywood North. *Vancouver Sun*, p. C4, Queue.

Caldwell, J. T. (2008). *Production culture.* Durham: Duke University Press.

California Assembly Bill 3114. (1976).

California Assembly Bill 2589. (1986).

California Assembly Bill 3066. (1986).

California Assembly Bill 3312. (1986).

California Assembly Bill 3555. (1986).

California Assembly Bill 7. (1987).

California Senate Bill 1189. (1975).

California Senate Bill 1620. (1976).

California State Senate. (1984). Motion Picture, Television, and Commercial Industries Act, §1639.

Canadian Audio-Visual Certification Office. (2004, February). *CPTC: Canadian film or video production tax credit.* Retrieved December 27, 2009, from Department of Canadian Heritage: http://www.pch.gc.ca/pgm/bcpac-cavco/pgm/cipc-cptc/pubs/guidec-eng.pdf.

Canadian Audio-Visual Certification Office . (2004, February). *PSTC: Film or video production services tax credit.* Retrieved December 27, 2009, from Department of Canadian Heritage: http://www.pch.gc.ca/pgm/bcpac-cavco/pgm/cisp-pstc/pubs/guide-eng.pdf.

Canclini, N. (1995). *Hybrid cultures: Strategies for entering and leaving modernity.* Minneapolis: University of Minnesota Press.

Canto, V. A. (1983/84, Winter). U.S. trade policy: History and evidence. *Cato Journal*, pp. 679–703.

Cartoonists end 9 1/2 week strike. (1982, October 11). *Los Angeles Times*, p. C4.

Christopherson, S. (2005). Divide and conquer: Regional competition in a concentrated media industry. In G. Elmer, & M. Gasher (Eds.), *Contracting out Hollywood: Runaway production and foreign location shooting* (pp. 21–40). Lanham, MD: Rowman & Littlefield.

——— (2009). Behind the scenes: How transnational firms are constructing a new international division of labor in media work (2006). In T. Miller (Ed.), *The contemporary Hollywood reader* (pp. 185–204). London: Routledge.

Christopherson, S., & Clark, J. (2007). *Remaking regional economies: Power, labor, and firm strategies in the knowledge economy.* New York: Routledge.

Christopherson, S., & Rightor, N. (2010). The creative economy as "big business": Evaluating state strategies to lure filmmakers. *Journal of Planning Education and Research, 29* (3), 336–352.

Christopherson, S., & Storper, M. (1989). The effects of lexible specialization on industrial politics and the labor market: The motion picture industry. *Industrial and Labor Relations Review, 42* (3), 331–347.

Conley Ulich, P., & Simmens, L. (2001). Motion picture production: To run or stay made in the U.S.A. *Loyola of Los Angeles Entertainment Law Review, 21*, 357–370.

Crabtree, S. (2004, April 19). Unions, pol face off over runaway production. *Variety*, p. 2, News.

Culhane, J. (1987, December 27). An animated '88 awaits on the drawing board. *New York Times*, pp. H31; 33.

Curtin, M. (2003). Media Capitals: Toward the study of spatial flows. *Journal of Cultural Sudies, 6* (2), pp. 202–28.

Cuthbert, P. (1996, April 8). Copps' cultural balancing act. *Playback*, p. 1.

Dales, J. L. (1971, March 20). Film tax incentive measure. *Los Angeles Times*, p. A4.

Dart, P. (1966, January 12). Wyler will shift to films abroad. *New York Times*, p. 27.

Dawson, A. (2006). "Bring Hollywood home!": Studio labour, nationalism and internationalism, and opposition to "runaway production," 1948–2003. *Revue Belge de Philologie & d'Histoire, 84* (4), pp. 1101–22.

Dinoff, D. (2006). Alberta back on Oscar Mountain. *Playback*, p. 28.

DiOrio, C. (2001, June 1). Valenti channels ire at broadband dearth. *Variety*, p. 4, News.

Dougherty, P. (1972, October 30). Advertising: "Runaways" in TV. *New York Times*, p. 50.

Douglas, K. (1960, December). All roads lead to . . . Hollywood. *The Journal of the Screen Producers Guild*, pp. 5–6.

Duara, P. (1996). Historicizing national identity, or who imagines what and when. In G. Eley, & R. G. Suny (Eds.), *Becoming national* (pp. 151–78). New York: Oxford University Press.

du Gay, P. (2000). Representing "Globalization": Notes on the discursive orderings of economic life. In P. Gilroy, L. Grossberg, & A. McRobbie (Eds.), *Without guarantees: In honour of Stuart Hall* (pp. 113–125). London: Verso.

Dunne, P. (1961, November 14). Griffith Park is not Enough. *Hollywood Reporter: 31st Anniversary Issue*.

Eckstein, A. (2004). The Hollywood Ten in history and memory. *Film History*, *16*, 424–36.

Economic impact study of the film industry in California. (1989). Los Angeles: California Chamber of Commerce and the California Film Commission.

Economics, not patriotism. (1961, December 6). *Variety*, p. 3.

Editorial: Losing the plot in "Hobbit" row. (2010, October 3). *New Zealand Herald*. Retrieved January 5, 2017 from: http://www.nzherald.co.nz/nz/news/article.cfm?c_id=1&objectid=10677758.

Edwards, I. (2002, March 18). Production to runaway beyond Canada. *Playback*, p. 10, News.

Elmer, G., & Gasher, M. (2005). *Contracting out Hollywood*. Lanham, MD: Rowman & Littlefield.

Ferguson, K. (2005, April 11). Time to rethink Canada's role as a production center. *Playback*, p. 12, Opinion.

Fighting runaway production: Madison Avenue rally. (1972–73, Winter). *The Bulletin of the International Alliance of Theatrical Stage Employes and Moving Picture Machine Operators of the United States and Canada*, pp. 3–4.

Film Council threatens boycott of foreign-made television pix. (1952, July 9). *Hollywood Reporter*, pp. 1, 8.

Film Council asks ban on import of Red movies. (1952, August 26). *Los Angeles Times*, p. 20.

Film Council asks U.S. act on British quotas. (1949, April 8). *Los Angeles Times*, p. A2.

Film unions seek federal subsidy. (1963, March 14). *Los Angeles Times*, p. 2.

Fiske, J. (1987). *Television culture*. New York: Routledge.

Foreign kickback on AFL ban. (1953, February 13). *Variety*, pp. 1, 13.

Fritz, B. (1999, August 16). Thousands march to fight runaway production. *Variety*, p. 1.

Funke, P. (1974, September 22). How you gonna keep 'em down in Hollywood after they've seen the sticks? *New York Times*, p. 135.

Gains small for British film talks. (1950, May 22). *Los Angeles Times*, p. B10.

Garrigues, G. (1966, July 28). Film studio gets OK for helistop. *Los Angeles Times*, p. WS1.
Gendel, M. (1986, December 8). Canada advantage: Budget TV. *Los Angeles Times*, pp. SD–D1.
Gerbner, G., & Gross, L. (1976). Living with television: The violence proile. *Journal of Communication, 26*, pp. 172–99.
Gitlin, T. (1980). *The whole world is watching.* Berkeley: University of Caliornia Press.
Gladstone, M. (1985, February 3). Officials hope to keep California in movie spotlight. *Los Angeles Times*, p. A3.
Gomery, D. (1986). *The Hollywood studio system: A history.* New York: St. Marten's Press.
Gould, J. (1970, November 22). Was big business right and the union wrong? *New York Times*, p. 123.
Gov. Reagan wants Nixon's aid to end runaway production. (1971, September 9). *The Hollywood Reporter*, p. 1.
Greenwald, W. I. (1952, January). The control of foreign trade: A half-century of film trade with Great Britain. *The Journal of Business of the University of Chicago.*
Gris, H. (1960, December 25). Film-making abroad not so sunny. *Los Angeles Times*, p. F3.
Guback, T. (1969). *International film industry: Western Europe and America since 1945.* Bloomington: Indiana University Press.
——— (1976). Hollywood's international market. In T. Balio, *The American Film Industry* (pp. 387–409). Madison: University of Wisconsin Press.
Gunther Lessing lashes "dictatorial" American Legion, "selfish" AFL demands. (1953, January 23). *Variety*, pp. 1, 11.
Hall, S. (1996). The West and the rest: Discourse and power. In S. Hall, D. Held, D. Hubert, & K. Thompson (Eds.), *Modernity: An introduction to modern societies* (pp. 185–225). Oxford, UK: Blackwell.
——— (2000). Encoding, decoding. In S. During (Ed.), *The cultural studies reader* (pp. 507–17). London: Routledge.
Hansard HL Deb vol 154 col 1095–6 (6 April 1948) [Electronic version].
Harford, M. (1967, April 29). Alien star advantage criticized. *Los Angeles Times*, p. 16.
Harmetz, A. (1985, April 8). Hollywood competitors rise from Texas to the Carolinas. *New York Times*, p. A1.
Harris, K. (1986, August 21). Fallout from tax reform. *Los Angeles Times*, p. A1.
Hearings before the Subcommittee on the impact of imports and exports on American employment of the Committee on Education and Labor, House of Representatives, 87th Congress, 1st and 2nd Sessions. (1962). Washington, D.C.: U.S. Congress.
Heflin, V. (1962, November 20). "Runaway" of necessity. *Hollywood Reporter*.
Harvey, D. (1990). *The condition of postmodernity.* Malden, MA: Blackwell.
Hay, J. (2003). Unaided virtues: The (neo)liberalization of the domestic sphere and the new architecture of community. In J. Z. Bratich, J. Packer, & C. McCarthy

(Eds.), *Foucault, cultural studies and governmentality* (pp. 165–206). Albany: State University of New York Press.

Herman, E. S., & Chomsky, N. (2002). *Manufacturing consent.* New York: Pantheon.

History: 1970s (2003, September 15). *Advertising Age.* Available June 20, 2016 at: http://adage.com/article/adage-encyclopedia/history-1970s/98703/.

Hollywood labor won't back down vs. undue U.S. production abroad. (1950, May 3). *Variety*, pp. 5, 22.

Hopper, H. (1962, August 16). Universal aspect of films defended. *Los Angeles Times*, p. C8.

——— (1962, October 18). Liz publicity off; Burton's fame rises. *Chicago Tribune*, p. C3.

Hornblow accents inevitability of Hollywood's expanding global production. (1950, April 19). *Variety*, pp. 2, 55.

Horne, G. (2001). *Class struggle in Hollywood, 1930–1950.* Austin: University of Texas Press.

Hoskins, C., Finn, A., & McFayden, S. (1996). Television and film in a free international trade environment: U.S. dominance and Canadian responses. In E. McAnany, & K. T. Wilkinson (Eds.), *Mass media and free trade: NAFTA and the cultural industries* (pp. 63–91). Austin: University of Texas Press.

Howell, P. (2001, December 7). Runaway production in reverse. *Toronto Star*, p. 8, Sports.

Hulbert, D. (1984, September 2). Texas yields a bumper crop of movies. *New York Times*, p. H11.

IATSE (1948). Proceedings of the thirty-ninth convention of the International Alliance of Theatrical Stage Employes and Moving Picture Machine Operators of the United States and Canada, (pp. 222–29). Cleveland, OH.

——— (1950). Proceedings of the fortieth convention of the International Alliance of Theatrical Stage Employes and Moving Picture Machine Operators of the United States and Canada, (pp. 72–75; 200–1; 212–17). Detroit, MI.

——— (1952). Proceeding of the forty-first convention of the International Alliance of Theatrical Stage Employes and Moving Picture Machine Operators of the United States and Canada, (pp. 178–83; 296–97). Minneapolis, MN.

——— (1956). Proceedings of the forty-third convention of the International Alliance of Theatrical Stage Employes and Moving Picture Machine Operators of the United States and Canada, (pp. 320–23). Kansas City, MO.

——— (1966). Proceedings of the forty-eighth convention of the International Alliance of Theatrical Stage Employes and Moving Picture Machine Operators of the United States and Canada. Detroit, MI.

——— (2000). *The second Golden Age, 1988–??* Retrieved June 26, 2010, from Animation Guild: http://www.animationguild.org/_Info/Info_h/_history_h/HISTORY9.HTM.

Illinois Department of Commerce and Equal Opportunity. (2009). *Tax incentive*. Retrieved March 15, 2009, from http://www.commerce.state.il.us/dceo/Bureaus/Film/Tax+Incentives/new+credit+-5-1.htm.

Johnston, Brewer reach no boycott conclusion. (1953, February 13). *Variety* , p. 1.

Jones, J. (1976, April 11). One-Stop permits aid L.A. movie makers. *Los Angeles Times*, pp. C1, C3.
Joseph, R. (1967, April 30). Tapping San Francisco's film potential. *Los Angeles Times*, pp. C16, 22.
Jowett, C. (2009, March 5). Take two for Hollywood North; 'Back On Radar'; Toronto's film industry making comeback. *National Post (Canada)*, p. A11.
Kaminsky, R. (1972, December 11). Georgia governor, delegation laud state, woo filmmakers. *Hollywood Reporter*, p. 11.
Kelly, B. (2002, July 22–28). Shooting slows in major cities. *Variety*, p. 14, International.
——— (2002, October 23). City to play role of N.Y. *Montreal Gazette*, pp. D1, Arts & Life.
——— (2007, September 21). Film industry sees drama in the making; Loss of revenue U.S. producers might stay home. *The Gazette (Montreal)*, p. B2.
——— (2008, January 21). Rising loony, strike hobble Toronto Studio's Startup. *Variety*, p. 10.
Kerlow, I. (2004). *The art of 3D computer animation and effects.* Hoboken, NJ: Wiley & Sons.
King, L. (1967, August 13). Don't call him senator soft-shoe. *Chicago Tribune*, p. I22.

King, V. (1953, October 26). Portrait of Roy M. Brewer. *The Hollywood Reporter: Anniversary Issue.*
——— (1965, August 6). SAG quits AFL film council. *The Hollywood Reporter*, pp. 1, 13.
Kirk, C. (1973, October 29). Peckinpah lashed on runaway. *Hollywood Reporter*, pp. 1, 4.
Knelman, M. (2003, September 27). Will Arnold kill Hollywood North? *Toronto Star*, p. A03, News.
Kraidy, M. (2005). *Hybridity, or the cultural logic of globalization.* Philadelphia: Temple University Press.
Labor whips "runaway" vipix. (1953, February 11). *Variety*, pp. 1, 13.
Lefebvre, H. (1991). *The production of space.* London: Blackwell.
Lehman, E. (1962, October 23). How to stop "runaway" productions. *Variety: Twenty-Ninth Anniversary Issue*, p. 49.
Lehners, J. W. (1970, October 27). "Runaway" production: Now 20 years old, but still labor's No. 1 concern. *149 (37)*, pp. 56, 58, 60.
Leisen, M. (1954, November 12). The dissidents abroad. *Hollywood Reporter: 24th Anniversary Issue*, section 2.
Lembke, D. (1963, June 19). Brown kills tax break for movie industry. *Los Angeles Times*, p. 14.
Lessing charges Brewer is usurping powers of "judge, jury & sheriff." (1953, January 27). *Variety*, pp. 1, 11.
Lewis, J. (1961, December 6). Embargo no cure for Hollywood. *Variety*, pp. 3, 22.
Loeb, P. (2007, July 26). *Simpsons got a little bit of Seoul.* Retrieved January 8, 2017, from American Public Media: Marketplace: https://www.marketplace.org/2007/07/26/life/simpsons-got-little-bit-seoul.

Lotz, A. (2007). *The television will be revolutionized.* New York: New York University Press.

Luther, C. (1984, January 8). Across the country: Hollywood's dollars go on location. *Los Angeles Times*, p. OC1.

MacDonald, G. (2003, May 28). Toronto's rough cuts. *The Globe and Mail*, p. R1, Globe Review Business.

MacMinn, A. (1968, August 20). Island action: Jack Lord finds job with Hawaii. *Los Angeles Times*, p. F17.

——— (1968, August 21). Ideal location: Boone an activist for Hawaii films. *Los Angeles Times*, p. F21.

Madigan, N. (1999, July 7). Hollywood invades capitol to halt runaway production. *Variety*, p. 2.

Malkki, L. (1996). National geographic: The rooting of peoples and the territorialization of national identity among scholars and refugees. In G. Eley, & R. G. Suny (Eds.), *Becoming national* (pp. 434–55). New York: Oxford University Press.

Margulies, L. (1986, September 23). Previewing the new fall season. *Los Angeles Times*, p. G10.

Marx, S. (1968, March). Shoot it in Griffith Park. *Journal of the Screen Producers Guild*, pp. 9–10, 15.

Massey, D. (1984). *The spatial divisions of labour.* London: MacMillan.

——— (1994). *Space, place, and gender.* Minneapolis: University of Minnesota Press.

Matheson, S. (2005). Projecting placelessness: Industrial television and the "authentic" Canadian city. In Elmer & Gasher (Eds). *Contracting out Hollywood* (pp. 117–39). Lanham, MD: Rowman & Littlefield.

McCullough, M. (2003, September 6). Arnie boasts he yanked T3 from Vancouver. *Vancouver Sun*, p. I1, Business.

McGrew, A. (1996). A global society? In S. Hall, D. Held, D. Hubert, & K. Thompson (Eds.), *Modernity: An introduction to modern societies* (pp. 466–503). Cambridge, MA: Blackwell Publishing.

McKay, J. (2006, March 3). Oscar's Canadian Connection. *Toronto Star*, p. E09.

McLellan, D. (2006, September 23). Roy M. Brewer, 97; Powerful figure during blacklist. *Los Angeles Times*, p. Metro, B12.

McNamara, L. (2001, August 8). "Chilly" Vancouver called unsuitable for Pasadena. *Vancouver Sun*, pp. B9, Entertainment.

McNary, D. (2001, December 4). Gilbert outlines plan to enforce Rule One. *Daily Variety*, pp. 8, News.

Meisler, S. (1973, December 14). Local controversy: Peckinpah film under union fire. *Los Angeles Times*, p. F26.

Mendelson, S. (2016, May 25). As 'X-Men: Apocalypse' opens, every 'X-Men' movie ranked from worst to best. *Forbes*. Retrieved January 7, 2017 from: http://www.forbes.com/sites/scottmendelson/2016/05/25/as-x-men-apocalypse-opens-every-x-men-movie-ranked-from-worst-to-best/#60b0fd86580e.

Metropolitan: 7 Americans held in stock plot. (1971, November 12). *Los Angeles Times*, p. A2.

Miller, T. (2003). The film industry and the government: "Endless Mr. Bonds and Mr. Beans?" In J. Lewis, & T. Miller (Eds.), *Critical cultural policy studies: A reader* (pp. 134–42). Malden, MA: Blackwell.

Miller, T., Govil, N., McMurria, J., & Maxwell, R. (2001). *Global Hollywood.* London: BFI Publishing.

Miller, T., & Leger, M. C. (2001). Runaway production, runaway consumption, runaway citizenship: The new international division of cultural labor. *Emergences, 11* (1), pp. 89–115.

Mitchell, C. (2004, October 30). big chill in Hollywood North. *The Toronto Star*, p. D11, Careers.

Monitor Company, The. (1999). *U.S. runaway film and television production study report.* Retrieved December 28, 2009, from http://www.hhill.org/images/uploads/monitor_report.pdf.

Monk, K. (2002, May 11). B.C.'s talent pool spills over. *Vancouver Sun*, p. D7, Mix.

——— (2003, May 2). Leaving L.A. for a reason. *Vancouver Sun*, p. D3, Arts & Life.

More Canadians invade American TV. (2002, July 27). *Toronto Star*, p. H15, Arts.

Morgan, J. (2001, February 24). Despite U.S. protests, B.C.'s film industry expands to 1.18 billion. *Vancouver Sun*, p. F2, Business.

Morley, D. (2001). Belongings: Place, space and identity in a mediated world. *European Journal of Cultural Studies, 4* (4), pp. 425–48.

Morris, M. (1988). At Henry Parkes Motel. *Cultural Studies, 2* (1), pp. 1–47.

Mosco, V. (2006). Knowledge and media workers in the global economy: Antimonies of outsourcing. *Social Identities, 12* (6), pp. 771–90.

Motion Picture Association of America (MPAA). (2015). *Theatrical market statistics.* Retrieved November 16, 2016 from http://www.mpaa.org/wp-content/uploads/2016/04/MPAA-Theatrical-Market-Statistics-2015_Final.pdf.

Motion Picture Development Unit. (1974). *Statutes of the State of California, §1226.* California.

MPIC revives anti-Red plan: Brewer's quitting IA cues need for new clarification program in ex-communists. (1953, September 22). *Hollywood Reporter*, pp. 1, 3.

MPIC to hear report tonight as foreign production topic boils. (1953, January 22). *Variety*, p. 3.

Mullen, M.G. (2008). *Television in the multichannel age: A brief history of cable television.* Malden, MA: Wiley-Blackwell.

Negus, K., & Román-Velázquez, P. (2000). Globalization and cultural identities. In J. Curran, & M. Gurevitch (Eds.), *Mass media and society* (pp. 329–45). New York: Oxford University Press.

Neil Craig and Associates. (2004, October). *International film and television production in Canada: Setting the record straight about U.S. "runaway" production.* Retrieved December 27, 2009, from http://www.filmontario.ca/documents/InternationalFilmTelevisionProductioninCanada.pdf.

Newman, J. (1989). Runaway production: Home is where the shot is. *Hollywood Reporter: 59th Anniversary Edition*, pp. 80, 84.

Nixon nixes Hollywood relief. (1971, April 6). *Hollywood Reporter*, p. 1.

Once and for all. (1952, September 30). *Variety.*

Ornstein, B. (1971, July 7). Cartoonists act on runaway. *The Hollywood Reporter*, pp. 1, 7.

Ostrow, R. (1963, June 4). Movie industry relief bill voted. *Los Angeles Times*, p. B7.

Ouellette, L. (2002). *Viewers like you? How public TV failed the people.* New York: Columbia University Press.

Packer, J. (2003). Disciplining mobility. In J. Bratich, C. McCarthy, & J. Packer (Eds.), *Foucault, Cultural Studies, and Governmentality* (pp. 135–61). Albany: State University of New York Press.

Patterson, F. T. (1930, February 5). Will Hollywood move to Broadway? *The New Republic*, pp. 297–99.

Paul, D. (2009, September 9). In Michigan, dream factories aim to replace auto sites. *New York Times*, p. 6.

Pendakur, M. (1990). *Canadian dreams and American control: The political economy of the Canadian film industry.* Detroit: Wayne State University Press.

Perkins, T. (1959, November 16). Authentic backgrounds are mor ethan an asset. *The Hollywood Reporter: 29th Anniversary Issue.*

Perlberg, W. (1960, December). What do you mean? Runaway production! *The Journal of the Screen Producers Guild*, pp. 7–8, 33.

Pieterse, J. N. (2004). *Globalization and culture: Global melange.* Lanham, MD: Rowman & Littlefield.

Piore, M. & Sabel, C. (1984). *The second industrial divide.* New York: Basic Books.

Plans offered to lessen "runaway" film output. (1962, April 17). *Los Angeles Times*, p. 32.

Plot Hollywood's "Greatest Story": Stevens talks with unions on making pic entirely here could ease "runaway" tension. (1962, May 11). *Variety*, pp. 1, 4.

Political and Economic Planning (PEP) (1952, May). *The British Film Industry: A report on its history and present organization, with special reference to the economic problems of British feature film production.* London.

Pollock, D. (1984, May 22). French and U.S. experts debate movie imports. *Los Angeles Times*, p. G1.

Powell, B. (2000, July 6). "Hollywood North" report iced in U.S. *Toronto Star*, p. 1, Entertainment.

Producers pick "My Fair Lady." (1965, March 9). *Chicago Tribune*, p. A4.

Pryor, T. (1953, June 7). Hollywood blues: Labor leaders seek tax change to stem talent exodus and production drop. *New York Times*, p. X5.

——— (1953, December 11). Studios explain filming abroad. *New York Times*, p. 42.

——— (1956, April 2). Extras threaten to end contract. *New York Times*, p. 18.

——— (1956, Sepetmber 2). Hollywood afield. *New York Times*, p. X5.

——— (1961, November 15). "Runaway" runaround crisis. *Variety*, pp. 1, 4.

——— (1961, November 16). Many roads open to "runaway" trend; all lead to dead-end for Hollywood. *Variety*, pp. 1, 4.

——— (1961, November 17). Deeper the "runaway" problem as deeper survey delves. *Variety*, pp. 1, 4.

Puette, W. J. (1992). *Through jauniced eyes: How the media view organized labor.* Ithaca, NY: ILR Press.

Randle, K., & Culkin, N. (2005). Still "a perfect world for capital"? Hollywood in an era of globalizing film production. *23rd Annual International Labor Process Conference, University of Strathclyde.*

Reguly, E. (2004, March 9). Runaway film work running away. *Globe and Mail*, pp. B2, Business.

Repeal of section 116 (a) (2) of the Internal Revenue Code, which excludes from gross income the amounts earned outside the United States by certain citizens of the United States, H.R. 4544, 83d Cong. (1953).

Rosen, H. (2001, September 17). The producer's chair. *Playback*, p. 8, News.

Ross, M. (1941). *Stars and strikes: Unionization of Hollywood.* New York: Columbia University Press.

Ross, S. (1998). *Working-class Hollywood.* Princeton, NJ: Princeton University Press.

Ruccio, D. (2008). *Economic representations: Academic and everyday*. New York: Routledge.

"Run-away" foreign film production irks AFL Council. (1952, July 9). *Variety*, p. 5.

"Runaway film" foreign wage pact formed. (1963, January 24). *Los Angeles Times*, p. A1.

"Runaway" film joint committee broken up. (1964, February 27). *Los Angeles Times*, p. 22.

Sassen, S. (2000). Spatialities and temporalities of the global: Elements for theorization. *Public Culture, 12* (1), pp. 215–32.

Saunders, D. (2001, March 30). The myth of Hollywood North. *Globe and Mail*, p. 94, Business Magazine.

Schiller, D. (2000). *Digital capitalism: Networking the global market system.* Cambridge, MA: MIT Press.

Schiller, H. (1969). *Mass communications and American empire.* Boulder, CO: Westview Press.

——— (1976). *Communication and cultural dominatio.* White Plains, NY: International Arts and Sciences Press.

Schumach, M. (1959, October 4). Hollywood stand. *New York Times*, p. X7.

Scott, A. (2002). A new map of Hollywood: the production and distribution of American motion pictures. *Regional Studies, 36* (9), pp. 957–75.

——— (2005). *On Hollywood: The place, the industry.* Princeton, NJ: Princeton University Press.

Scott, A., & Pope, N. (2007). Hollywood, Vancouver, and the world: Employment relocation and the emergence of satellite production centers in the motion-picture industry. *Environment and Planning, 39*, pp. 1364–81.

Segrave, K. (1999). *Movies at home: How Hollywood came to television*. Jefferson, NC: McFarland & Company.

Self-searching in the movies. (1962, November 15). *Los Angeles Times*, p. A4.

Shanks, H. O., Lehners, J., & Gilbert, R. (1961, December 18). Letters to the Times: Hollywood Council officers deny making headline-hunting attack. *Los Angeles Times*, p. B5.

Sherman, G. (1961, November 27). Exodus of film makers fades Hollywood's glitter. *Los Angeles Times*, p. B1.

Shohat, E., & Stam, R. (1994). *Unthinking Eurocentricism: Multiculturalism and the media.* London: Routledge.

Show business: It just ain't so. (1980, April 21). Retrieved August 8, 2010, from Time: http://www.time.com/time/magazine/article/0,9171,924015,00.html.

Shrimpton, J. (2006, February 25). Wyoming's double take: The sweeping vistas of Brokeback Mountain purport to be Wyoming but they're actually a cheap imitation. *Townsville Bulletin.*

Siegel brands IA beef "outside" SPG domain. (1953, January 20). *Variety*, pp. 1, 17.

Singleton, S. (2010, August 28). Film industry thrives. *Toronto Sun*, p. 35.

Sinoski, K. (2016, April 8). Boom time for residents, businesses in Hollywood North. *Vancouver Sun*. Available June 20, 2016 at: http://vancouversun.com/news/local-news/boom-time-for-residents-businesses-in-hollywood-north.

Sito, T. (2006). *Drawing the line: The untold story of the animation unions from Bosko to Bart Simpson.* Lexington: University of Kentucky Press.

Smith, C. (1964, June 15). Movies coming back, but far from old peak. *Los Angeles Times*, p. F7.

——— (1964, June 16). Credit for new vigor in studios goes to TV. *Los Angeles Times*, p. E7.

Smith, M. (1998). Theses on the history of Hollywood history. In S. Neale & M. Smith (Eds.), *Contemporary Hollywood cinema* (pp. 3–20). London: Routledge.

Sokoloff, H. (2002, March 4). Hollywood riven by union fight. *National Post (Canada)*, p. A3, News.

Spigel, L. (1992). *Make room for television.* Chicago: University of Chicago Press.

Spiro, J. (1950, April 9). Hollywood peace: Johnston placates labor anent foreign production—selling big business. *New York Times*, p. X5.

——— (1952, August 3). Hollywood Dossier: Unions set campaign against "runaway" movies production overseas—addenda. *New York Times*, p. X3.

State federation opens convention. (1955, August 15). *New York Times*, p. 35.

Steiger, P. (1970, November 9). Movie fund may dump Mobil stock over British TV grant. *New York Times*, p. D11.

Storper, M. (1994). The transition to flexible specialisation in the US film industry: External economies, the division of labour and the crossing of industrial divides. In Amin, A. (Ed.). *Post-Fordism: A reader* (pp. 195–226). Oxford, UK: Blackwell Publishers.

Stubbs, J. (2008). "Blocked" currency, runaway production in Britain and Captain Horatio Hornblower (1951). *Historical Journal of Film, Radio and Television, 28* (3), pp. 335–51.

Sullivan, J. (2008). Marketing creative labor: Hollywood "making of" documentary features (pp. 69–83). Mosco, V. & McKercher, C. (Eds.). *Knowledge Workers in the Information Society*. Lanham, MD: Lexington Books.

Sutherland, H. (1968, February 9). See foreigners stealing show, critics pan New York's prospects as film center. *Los Angesles Times*, p. A6.

Thompson, K. (1985). *Exporting entertainment: America in the world film market, 1907–1934*. London: British Film Institute.

Thrifty Drug yields to AFL campaign against foreign vidpix; union clears "Hans." (1953, February 4). *Variety*, pp. 1, 10.

Tinic, S. (2006). Global vistas and local reflections: Negotiating place and identity in Vancouver television. *Television and New Media, 7* (2), pp. 154–83.

Tolusso, S. (2001, February 5). Tax credit where due. *Playback*, pp. 6, Editorial.

Townsend, D. (1979, August 25). Striking TV cartoonists return to drawing boards. *Los Angeles Times*, p. A27.

Tribune series will tell the woes of "Cleopatra." (1963, June 21). *Chicago Tribune*, p. 2.

Tuchman, G. (1978). *Making news: A study in the construction of reality.* Free Press.

Tusher, W. (1972, March 27). Mexico lures TV commercials. *Hollywood Reporter*, pp. 1, 22.

——— (1974, July 5). Arizona new champ of runaway states. *Hollywood Reporter*, pp. 1, 10.

U.S. Bureau of the Census. (1930). *General report on occupations.* Washington, D.C.: U.S. Government Printing Office.

U.S. Department of Commerce. (2001, January). *The migration of U.S. film and television production.* Retrieved December 28, 2009, from http://www.ita.doc.gov/media/migration11901.pdf.

U.S. International Trade Commission. (2001, May). *Recent trends in U.S. services trade*. Retrieved Sepetember 8, 2010, from http://www.usitc.gov/publications/docs/pubs/332/PUB3409.pdf.

U.S. leaders in London for Film Pact discussion. (1950, May 14). *Los Angeles Times*, p. D2.

Unions to help film producers fight tariff. (1949, March 7). *Los Angeles Times*, p. A1.

Vagnini, S. (2009, May 1). *News & features: Hooray for Hollywood.* Retrieved June 20, 2010, from D23: The official community for Disney fans: http://d23.disney.go.com/articles/050109_NF_FS_DisneyMGM.html.

Vamos, P. (2004, September 13). Runaway production a fair trade. *Playback*, p. 14, News.

Wachs, J. (1975). Hollywood: Cityside. *The Hollywood Reporter: 45th Anniversary Edition*, 12.

Wanger, W. and Hyams, J. (1963). *My Life with Cleopatra: The Making of a Hollywood Classic*. New York: Vintage Books.

Wasko, J. (2001). *Understanding Disney.* Malden, MA: Blackwell.

——— (2003). *How Hollywood Works.* London: Sage.

——— (2008). Financing and production: Creating the Hollywood film community. In P. McDonald, & J. Wasko (Eds.), *The contemporary Hollywood film industry* (pp. 43–62). Malden, MA: Blackwell.

Wasser, F. (2001). *Veni, vidi, video.* Austin: University of Texas.

Waterman, D. (1982). The structural development of the motion picture industry. *American Economist*, *26*(1), pp. 16–27.

Waters, M. (2001). *Globalization (2nd Ed.).* New York: Routledge.

Waters, T. (1979, August 11). 800 film cartoonists threaten strike. *Los Angeles Times*, p. A20.

——— (1980, July 14). Postscript: Out-of-work U.S. cartoonists still fight foreign competition. *Los Angeles Times*, p. C1.

Waters, T., & Bernstein, H. (1979, August 15). Idle cartoonists: Back to drawing board? *Los Angeles Times*, p. SD10.

Weiler, A. (1960, January 20). Movie maker hires blacklisted writer. *New York Times*, p. 1.

Wells, P. (2003). "Smarter than the average art form": Animation in the television era. In C. A. Stabile, & M. Harrison (Eds.), *Prime time animations: Television animation and American culture* (pp. 15–32). London: Routledge.

Williams, D. (1961, December 3). Hollywood's woe: Runaway, fadeaway. *Los Angeles Times*, p. A5.

Williams, R. (2003). *Television: Technology and cultural form (3rd ed.).* New York: Routledge.

Wilson, J. M. (1986, May 18). Outtakes: Fire sale. *Los Angeles Times*, p. Q20.

Windeler, R. (1968, January 8). Hollywood: It's lively for a ghost town. *New York Times*, p. 127.

——— (1969, January 6). Movie gains up as barriers fall. *New York Times*, p. 131.

Wirtz appoints board on "runaway" films. (1963, January 25). *Los Angeles Times*, p. 18.

Wood, D. (2009, March 2). California moves to hold onto Hollywood. *Christian Science Monitor*, p. 3.

Wright, R. (1970, December 6). Filming abroad scored by unions. *New York Times*, p. 84.

Yaffe, S. (2002, January 8). 2002: The year of the coproduction. *Playback*, p. 4, Editorial.

——— (2002, March 4). Canada vs. US. *Playback*, pp. 4, Editorial.

Yoon, H., & Malecki, E. J. (2009). Cartoon planet: Worlds of production and global production networks in the animation industry. *Industrial and Corporate Change, 19* (1), pp. 239–71.

Zanuck, D. F. (1960, December). Shoot it where you find it! *The Journal of the Screen Producers Guild*, pp. 3–4; 31.

Index

About the Author

Camille Johnson-Yale is an assistant professor of Communication at Lake Forest College. As a specialist in critical media studies, her research interests include media industries, media labor and policy studies, new media and communication technologies, and media history. Her work has appeared in several publications, including *Critical Studies in Media Communication*, *Journal of Popular Culture*, *New Media & Society*, *The Pew Internet and American Life Project*, and *American Reception Study: Reconsiderations and new directions.* Among the accolades Dr. Johnson-Yale has received for her work, she was given top honors by the Association of Internet Researchers and named one of the "New Voices in Critical and Cultural Studies" by the National Communication Association. Before entering academia, Dr. Johnson-Yale worked in the television and motion picture production industries in Chicago. She remains connected with the Chicago production community through her husband, Robert, who has been an active member of IATSE 476 for over twenty years.

CPSIA information can be obtained
at www.ICGtesting.com
Printed in the USA
BVOW04*2100010517
482666BV00001B/1/P

9 781498 532532